"Success after all is only a collection of many good results. This book tells us how to get them. A breakthrough in modern marketing."

> – **Bob Proctor**, Master Success Coach, Best Selling Author, Teacher in *"The Secret"*

"This timely, relevant and energizing digital marketing book reminds us of a simple truth. When marketing feels personal to the consumer, it is welcomed. Making your messaging and experience all about your customer rather than your brand leads to happy clients and a successful business. This book is a must-read for any business looking to create deeper connections with its customers."

> – **Peggy McColl**, *New York Times* Best Selling Author

"As I've said before, your customers don't care about you, your products or your services. They care about themselves. This book explains why a YOU-centric approach is a must in today's marketing environment. Everyone who wants to be a successful marketer should read it."

> – **Joe Pulizzi**, Founder of Content Marketing Institute, author, marketing speaker, and entrepreneur

"**What's Working Now** is not a business book, it is a handbook for marketing in 2019. I found the book very refreshing. It is written by a real person with real marketing experience for other business people to put the material to immediate use. In contrast to other business books, 98% of this book contains tangible information you can use. It's not a thesis or the result of a decade long study. It is a simple, easy to read handbook about how to market your product to today's consumer using today's marketing tools. Simple as that. This book's intelligence is in its simplicity and usefulness. The book is strategic and is coupled with hands on ways to apply the strategies discussed. This book is the future of marketing."

> – **Blair Kellison**, CEO Traditional Medicinals

Published by
Hasmark Publishing
www.hasmarkpublishing.com

Disclaimer

This book is designed to provide information and motivation to our readers. It is sold with the understanding that the publisher is not engaged to render any type of psychological, legal, or any other kind of professional advice. The content of each article is the sole expression and opinion of its author, and not necessarily that of the publisher. No warranties or guarantees are expressed or implied by the publisher's choice to include any of the content in this volume. Neither the publisher nor the individual author(s) shall be liable for any physical, psychological, emotional, financial, or commercial damages, including, but not limited to, special, incidental, consequential or other damages. Our views and rights are the same: You are responsible for your own choices, actions, and results.

Permission should be addressed in writing to Shahla Hebets at shebets@thinkmediaconsult.com or 1520 S. Fillmore St., Denver CO 80210

Editor: Nita L. Robinson
www.NitaHelpingHand.com

Cover and Layout: Anne Karklins
anne@hasmarkpublishing.com

ISBN 13: 978-1-989161-81-4
ISBN 10: 1989161812

WHAT'S WORKING NOW?

YOU-centric Marketing

SHAHLA HEBETS

To my incredible children, Cameron and Devyn,
who always inspire me to be my best,
and to my amazing husband, Russell,
who believes that I can do anything.
Life is so much better with you.

Acknowledgements

This book would not be possible were it not for the relationships that I built at the start of my career through the support and guidance of Fred Linder and Scott Owen. Fred was my first mentor and teacher. He took me under his wing when I was new to business, client relationships and marketing, and taught me how to be a strong leader. Scott was my second mentor, and he showed me that being effective in any role starts with compassion, understanding and teamwork. I am eternally grateful to both.

I was equally guided by two additional inspiring and gracious mentors, Chuck Verde and Cynthia Davis. They repeatedly made time for phone calls and discussions over the years as well as helped guide the launch of my business in 2016. Their willingness to assist never wavered, and I'm blessed to call them both friends. Tom Joyce was another mentor who was tireless in his commitment to encourage my every move. To say that I have been fortunate to have many generous teachers would be an understatement, and I'm beyond thankful.

Another notable person worth mentioning is Joe Pulizzi. I worked with Joe many moons ago, and I have been watching his magnificent career from the sidelines. Joe provided me with a role model and example of where to aim my aspirations. Thank you!

Finally, I would like to acknowledge my parents, Bahman and Vernelle Hemmat, for their endless belief in me and for championing my every idea and inclination. There is nothing more valuable than knowing your family is in your corner. Your unconditional love makes all the difference.

I am beyond grateful to all for your love and support.

Contents

Introduction

What's working now in the world of digital marketing? It is a commonly asked question and it is of relevance, regardless of the industry that you are in, the size of the market, the competition, and whether you are a start-up or an established brand. Everyone wants to know what is actually working to increase qualified traffic to your website, to cultivate and build leads, to highlight your brand's uniqueness and create as well as sustain brand awareness that your company can be proud of, and the biggie – what actually generates sales? This question continues to be asked with good reason; the digital marketing environment has undergone a massive amount of change, influx, ebbs/flows and transformation over the past five to ten years alone.

More than that, many traditional and once hailed as "tried and true" digital marketing strategies and tactics no longer work. They have been so overused or misused that your brand either can't break through the proverbial clutter and marketing noise, or the consumer no longer values or trusts these measures. That has resulted in a lot of head scratching and fear that very little in the digital marketing world truly works today. The biggest reason for this prevailing thought is that most brands are simply copying what other brands are doing. They say, "Well, if it works for XYZ brand, it will work for us." However, that assumption is flawed because what works for other brands most likely *won't* work for you. Beyond that, it makes your brand virtually indistinguishable from other brands.

This homogeneity is one of the biggest challenges that all brands face in the ever-evolving, crowded ecosystem of digital marketing. How do you break out of a category where all brands are positioned similarly? The reality is that almost all market segments face the same challenge. In most cases, your brand and your competitors seem awfully similar in the eyes of the consumer.

One glaring example of this is in the health and wellness lifestyle product space, where all brands tout the virtues of their organic and natural ingredients, the health benefits, and so on. While this may be true for many products, these messages don't distinguish the brands from one another. It is a growing industry, but one only needs to walk into a natural food grocer to feel overwhelmed by the sea of product sameness. This is just one market example; there are examples of this in every market.

So what is working now? What works now is defining your product in terms of your customer, not in terms of your brand or competition. What works is figuring out what your customer values. What works is putting your humanistic or people-centric attributes first and your brand secondary or even tertiary (third on the list of priorities). What works is thinking strategically about your true purpose and shining a spotlight on that. What works is elevating your game to think big, act big and be big.

The good news is that there is much that is working now in the digital marketing landscape. It just takes a shift in focus, perspective and a willingness to forge your own unique path, and leave the copycats behind. Are you ready to hear more? Good, because there is much more to share. Before that, let me tell you a little about me.

A Little About Me

When I was a teenager and entering the part-time, after-school work environment, my dad would ask if I was giving 100% at work. When I would say yes, he would answer, "Good, but you need to give 150% if you want to be successful." This conversation shaped my thinking and has continued to guide my thoughts today. After 20 years of working with start-ups, small and medium sized businesses and giant multinational, multibillion dollar corporations, I have always given 150% (not to worry, Dad). That doesn't mean that I didn't have my setbacks, but it means that my commitment to achieving success has always been a high priority.

Throughout the early days of my career all the way up to today, one thing became crystal clear – I love helping companies grow their businesses and revenues. Although that might sound cliché, it is the truth. In 1998, I started selling trade show sponsorships to health and natural product companies. It was fun and creative, but what I really enjoyed was when my clients had a really successful sponsored event, seminar or other promotion. I took great pride in knowing that my efforts in matching them with the right opportunity (or more often creating the right opportunity) resulted in them meeting new customers, generating new leads and growing their business. One year later, I moved into selling print magazine advertisements, and I was afforded the opportunity to improve my clients' businesses over a full calendar year. What can I say? I was in love.

This love affair with marketing success has never wavered. After all these years of working in the digital marketing, multimedia environment, I still wake each morning eager to contribute to my clients' success. In the early years of my career, I worked with natural product brands many of which are top sellers today. In time, new opportunities for growth started to present themselves, and I was hired to run a multimedia division (online, events and print) in the convenience retail space. I moved out of the natural product, health and wellness industry and into the world of multinational powerhouse brands. Suddenly, I was overseeing large advertising and media strategies for some of the world's most beloved brands. It was both rewarding and challenging.

After a few years, opportunity knocked on my door again, and I was hired to oversee a struggling multimedia division in the audio and video technology industry. I worked with clients that are largely household names. From there, I moved into overseeing a division in the travel and hospitality field where I worked with large hotel brands before joining an ecommerce company where I oversaw one of their largest divisions. The short version is that I worked in multiple industries, with clients ranging from under a million dollars in revenue to clients generating billions in revenue. There isn't a form of digital marketing, sponsored content or advertising that I haven't worked with and overseen.

Throughout my corporate journey, I kept dreaming of something more, something bigger. I came up with what felt like a million business plans (Okay, more like half a dozen), but they never seemed quite right. Then, in the early summer of 2016, I made an official announcement to my family. I was going to start my own digital marketing consultancy business. I had a pit in my stomach as I proclaimed my intentions, but something inside of me knew that I was ready. Shortly after launching my business, I acquired my first client through a referral. Woot, woot! Not long after, I landed one of the top Fortune 100 companies as a client, then more followed. The rest, as they say, is history.

It is the experience that I gained assisting start-ups, small, medium, large and gigantic companies grow that gave me the inspiration and the real world, hands on experience to write this book. It has always been my ultimate vision to become an author and help even more people succeed. And BAM! I did it. It just goes to show that my motto is true: *Think big and big things happen.*

Chapter 1: **Expecting Success**

Before I started my own digital marketing consultancy business, I made a crucial decision that impacted every other aspect of my life. I mention it here because I believe that the lessons I learned from it are critical to your digital marketing success. On my 39th birthday, I decided that it was time to put into motion a higher vision of myself. That higher vision was floating around my dreams for years. I have always been someone who believed in accomplishing all that there is to achieve in this life, but despite my very real aspirations, I felt stuck. What was worse was that feeling of being stuck was starting to overshadow the other wonderful areas of my life. I needed some guidance, but I didn't know where to begin. Then, just like that, inspiration struck.

I was driving to work thinking about how I could move away from my limiting beliefs (although I didn't know they were called that at the time) and start living the life that I envisioned. Suddenly, I remembered that when I was 12 years old, my father had attended a seminar and several workshops from a company called PSI. This resulted in a major turning point in my father's life, but somehow it had been relegated to the forgotten areas of my mind in adulthood. When I arrived at work, I googled PSI Seminars, and lo and behold, the company, 27 years later, was still in existence and appeared to be thriving. PSI stands for Personal Success Institute, and upon reading the name, I thought, "Yes, this sounds like what I need." I read through the site and various reviews of the program.

Then I realized they had a seminar scheduled in Denver which was occurring over my birthday weekend. It was kismet. Still, I couldn't get past the seminar's price tag so I decided to give it some thought. For days, I repeatedly went back to the site and agonized with the decision. Finally, I decided to broach the subject with my husband and life partner (something always wise to do when making important decisions).

After speaking with my husband, I took what I felt was an incredible leap of faith and signed up for the seminar. At the time, the cost for the seminar seemed like a lot of money to spend. In hindsight, I think of it as one of the most nominal yet profound investments of my life. Fast forward, I ended up attending all three of the seminars that PSI Seminars offered. What I learned then and continue to learn, is that being successful in business (and in life) boils down to expecting success. *Right! I have heard that before,* you say? Well, dismiss it at your own peril because it is 100% true! Becoming successful is about having unwavering faith that your dreams are within reach. It is the belief that you are worthy and capable of living the life you want. This belief applies to the product or service that you sell because it starts and ends with you. The same applies to your marketing efforts. If your intention is to improve your customer's lives, then you will. If you believe that your business will be a smashing success and you put in the real work and action needed, it will be. If you approach each day with focus and an attitude of being of service and a positive contribution, you will create this reality. I have seen this firsthand in my own life so I know it can happen for you. Because what you think and act upon becomes your reality.

Chapter 2: **Grit**

Throughout my years of experience, I have noticed three prevailing thoughts with companies looking to grow their business through marketing. The first is the assumption that because they have a great product, little to no budget will suffice in getting the word out. They wrongly believe that they can use a grassroots approach which will yield immediate results. This assumption disregards the fact that this type of low budget, grassroots marketing is rooted most predominantly in time, and a lot of it. It takes lasting, undeterred effort with a focus on building one tribe member at a time until one day (and often many years of scraping by), the product reaches critical mass. Of course, there is the occasional exception, but typically, they are extremely rare; the stars effectively have to align. However, these business leaders tend to live in a world of fast decisions and fast results, and they understandably want the same for their company. They just don't understand the rarity of fast growth or, more specifically, fast growth without a sizable marketing budget.

The second assumption is that with the internet, all things are possible (which is true), but they assume that merely entering the worldwide web means people will suddenly flock to their site and purchase their product. They forget the importance of brand building. Here's the fundamental truth: You cannot skip brand building even if you wish it otherwise. One only needs to look at a very well-known, legacy beverage company to recognize that brand building pays off. They still spends tremendous amounts of marketing capital on branding, yet can you think of a more recognizable or iconic brand? A hugely popular and heavily branded technology company is another great example. Successful brands make continual branding a priority. But I digress. When I discuss branding, I mean building a strong brand and consistently delivering on your brand promise.

They also forget that the internet is an ever-growing, competitive marketplace where doing even many things right doesn't necessarily result in a thriving business. It takes work, dedication, action, commitment, knowledge (as well as a willingness to constantly learn) and an egoless obsession with change to ensure that you're meeting the customer's needs while adapting to their changing behaviors. In short, internet marketing is complex, and this complexity seems to be amplified by the day. This is where some business leaders fall down. They falsely assume that the internet is simply a door to be opened, and ignore the craftsmanship required in building the door to begin with, or how to earn a customer's trust such that they are willing to go through the door. They don't appreciate the truly competitive nature of the internet and the tenacity it takes to persevere in this competitive, ever-changing landscape.

The third misperception is that their goals are their customer's goals. I used to work for a company like this. They would say, "We want to roll out this product because it will increase our revenue." They didn't stop to think, *How does this product serve our customer? Do they actually want or need this?* Companies with this disposition focus exclusively on releasing a "new" product and ignore why the product matters to the consumer. They don't think of the customers as the end-all be-all of their brand. Instead, they think that if their product is new, different or otherwise, the customer will fall over themselves to understand and apply its benefits to themselves. They totally disregard the fact that the customer should easily understand why the product will improve their lives. They put little importance into communicating their brand's story or placing their customer's needs and wants far above their own.

In short, they treat their customers like a commodity, something to be gained through minimal effort. It is as though they feel they are doing the customer a favor by selling them their product. What this assumption fails to recognize is that the customer is king. They reign supreme and the brand needs to work to gain, retain and cultivate an on-going relationship with them. They think the YOU in YOU-centric marketing applies to the brand, not the customer. So let me make this perfectly clear: Your brand will never become a superstar brand until you realize what the "you" in YOU-centric actually means. It means: your customer, your customer's needs, your customer's wants, your customer's life, your customer's values, your customer's interests. If you understand this and begin applying it to your business, you will gain your customer's loyalty and your business will grow proportionately.

Chapter 3: **When Did Marketing Become So Hard?**

"When did marketing get so complicated and hard?" my client Joe asked me one morning over coffee. He was clearly frustrated by the new terms such as "content marketing," "social media influencers," "referral marketing" and everything in between. Joe was a hardworking business owner in the wellness industry. For years, his business grew by word of mouth. As a result, he did some marketing here and there, ran occasional TV ads, exhibited at some targeted events, and performed and engaged in some email marketing campaigns. He was generally happy with the performance and return on his investments. Until one day the referrals dried up and he found himself without any answers as to what went wrong. As his business waned, he started to investigate marketing options but felt overwhelmed by the choices and uncertainty. When he finally came to us, he was confused and disheartened.

So what did happen? Why did this once successful business powered by word of mouth (which is the Holy Grail in social media marketing) stop getting new customers? In truth, several things occurred. To begin with, his marketing efforts no longer connected with consumers. We have devoted a whole chapter on consumer behavior which will go into much more detail, but suffice it to say, his customers' needs and wants changed. Second, he got too comfortable. His reliance on referrals (while understandable) became his Achilles heel because he did very little additional marketing (not even social media marketing!) to engage his current customers or reach new customers. He hadn't given any thought to developing his company's story, let alone sharing it. In addition, he wrongly thought he didn't really need to engage in consistent marketing. Oh, if I had a dollar for every client that has expressed that same pervasive misconception. Third, his marketing efforts were primarily focused on traditional advertising methods which have undergone a whole host of disruption over the years, leading to steadily diminishing returns. Fourth, he hadn't stayed current on trends, new competition or other happenings in the fitness industry. Not only was he losing business, he was not at all well-versed as to where his customers were going. He was losing on multiple fronts all at once, which explained his notable frustration.

The marketing industry has experienced massive change in the past 10-15 years. The truth is that what once worked, largely no longer does, primarily because of the massive proliferation of media platforms. Think Facebook, Twitter, Instagram, Pinterest, YouTube, LinkedIn, Reddit, and Medium, just to name a few. And that doesn't factor in traditional channels such as TV, radio, newspapers, and magazines which are still capturing some attention, albeit far less than in the past. Add in Google, Yahoo, Bing, Netflix, Hulu, Pandora and other media companies/outlets, and it is a bit dizzying. The end result is that consumers now have a vast plethora of media choices, so capturing their attention for even a nanosecond can be challenging. Brands feel this too; they now have to find ways to communicate with their customers across a virtual universe of platforms, which is no small task.

Prior to this massive influx of new media outlets, companies like Joe's relied on a few tried and true means to reach their customers. Namely, they used TV (those who could afford it), radio, print, outdoor advertising, and their website to reach customers via search engine marketing (Google Ads) and search engine optimization. Most companies relied on a few and disregarded the others, but the big guys played in all. And it worked. They could connect with their target audience as they leisurely thumbed through their favorite magazine, reach people during their commute via the radio, and use search engines online such as Google and Bing to target people via relevant keywords. Their biggest focus was on the creation of captivating campaigns, knowing that the media outlets themselves would deliver millions of eyeballs (oh, the good ol' days). Then it all changed. Enter Facebook, February 2004. In the early days, Facebook's founder was focused on universities, but his aspirations quickly grew. By August 2008, Facebook had a million users and was off to the races in terms of capturing people's attention. Today, over two billion people use Facebook on a monthly basis. Now factor in the exceptional growth of other social platforms such as Twitter. Twitter launched in March 2006, and by 2009, Twitter had surpassed the five billion tweet mark (that's a lot of tweets!). YouTube launched in 2005, was purchased by Google in 2006, and it was estimated that by 2007, YouTube consumers had used as much bandwidth as the entire internet in 2000. So to say that YouTube grew quickly doesn't do it justice. Pinterest launched in March of 2010, and by January 2012 had 11.7 million users. On and on these disruptive social media networks have wiggled their way into the hearts and minds of consumers, and something had to give. That something turned out to be your advertising. There was simply no time to consume your advertising in the midst of all these other, far more interesting networks.

Because of the emergence of new media platforms, what followed was a lot of new avenues for brands to engage their customers. However, many brands (and when I say many, I mean almost all) continued to use the interruptive advertising tactics they had grown accustomed to in traditional channels. Imagine for a moment that you are a brand manager and suddenly your creative team has to create ads for all these new media platforms and networks in addition to your traditional media outlets. That is a big ask, so most brands just took the same formula and applied it to the new platform. That meant your target customer was seeing your ads, and many, many other ads, on every conceivable outlet, a lot more than they had previously. That led to ad fatigue (they got tired of seeing ads), and that fatigue ultimately resulted in the consumer's ability to simply tune out the advertisement and focus on messaging that felt "real" or "authentic." Thus, advertising blindness was born, a serious condition that impacts your ad performance. Consumers have willingly and purposefully gone out of their way to ignore your ad. And is it any wonder? It is incredibly easy to click out of a pop-up on a website, to skip the ad (or mentally tune out), fast forward through the commercial, scroll past the sponsored post in your social media feed, and on and on. Ads that feel like ads get overlooked. Joe's ads felt like ads, and that is why he was failing. They felt like a sales pitch. They didn't offer education, entertainment, inspiration or any of the elements needed to look or feel like anything other than an ad. They weren't relevant to the needs or wants of his customers. They weren't focused on his audience. They were focused on his brand. As a result, his ads were snubbed, and we already know the outcome it had on his business.

The good news is that marketers in today's environment don't need to give up. They just need to put their customer wants and needs first. Marketing assets should be viewed in terms of the value they can provide their target audience. Joe was in the wellness industry so instead of making a traditional pitch on why you needed to become a member, he could have created an ebook showcasing five fun and quick workouts that burn fat. He could have created a video series of tasty, metabolism-boosting recipes. He could have written blogs on the best hikes nearby. The list goes on and on. Now you are probably thinking that this seems like a lot of work – and it is, but so is creating sales materials that are never read, crafting ads that are never watched or consumed, and drafting email campaigns that are never opened. You get it, right? What Joe needed to do was to take a critical look at where he was spending his marketing efforts unsuccessfully and replace them with YOU-centric tactics that are successful. This is where the grit and commitment that was previously mentioned comes in. It takes a willingness to ask, *What does my target customer really need?* It takes a commitment to make your messaging all about your customer. And here's the rub: you can't fake it. It actually needs to be about providing real value to your customer long before they become your customer. If you're not sure how to do this, don't worry, I'm going to show you how.

Chapter 4: **What is YOU-centric Marketing?**

If you have heard the expression, *What's in it for me?* then you know exactly what YOU-centric marketing means. YOU-centric marketing asks the questions that all consumers ask when deciding to read, view, engage, interact, evaluate, and ultimately purchase your product or service. Specifically, they ask, *Why should I care? What will this product or service actually do for me? How will it benefit my health, beauty, reputation, knowledge, status, mood, etc.? How will it enhance my life or the lives of my family? Why should I bother? Will this make a difference? Is this even worth my time?* YOU-centric marketing aims to answer these questions before the consumer even thinks them by putting your value proposition into messaging that your customers actually care about.

YOU-centric marketing is genuine. It doesn't try to trick the customer into purchasing. The goal is not to deceive. It aims to provide authentic interactions through your content and communication. It aims to tell, convey and reinforce that your customer's needs, desires, wishes and wants are of the highest concern to your business. This means that not only do you have to understand your customer, you also have to make a commitment to provide them with the value and experience they seek. YOU-centric marketing should understand what your customer needs at each stage of the buying funnel – at the awareness, interest, consideration, intent, evaluation and purchase levels – and fulfill that need. Therefore, it requires thought and evaluation. It requires a willingness to see the shifts in your target customer's behaviors and provide new and interesting ways to connect and engage with them.

Most of all, it requires that the needs of your business are not the driving force of your customer interactions. This doesn't mean your company's revenue goals, etc. should be dismissed, but it does mean that this isn't about you. It is about your audience and their needs. YOU-centric marketing is built on the fundamental truth that your customer will make or break your company, so ignoring the reality of their thoughts, interests, needs, dreams, wants and desires will lead to the undoing of your business.

It seeks to understand the individual consumer, not the persona group. It looks at one person and seeks to understand what they read, who they respect (and follow), what their values are, their goals and aspirations, their challenges and obstacles, what their family dynamics are, and how that impacts their desires. You might think this sounds like an impossible task, but if you were to sit down and ask your neighbor some thought-provoking questions along these lines, you would quickly learn these answers and walk away with a monumentally new level of understanding about him/her. Once you do, you can deduce that there are many others that have similar aspirations as your neighbor. The same applies to your business. Interview some of your current customers or people that you wish were your current customers. Understand what they really want, need, admire and value. Understand their challenges and goals. Once you understand them as individuals – viola – your persona group is born! Now do this a few more times and suddenly you will have three to four customer personas that you can use to guide your content creation and targeting.

YOU-centric marketing is also about honoring your relationship with your customers. It is about treating them as they wish to be treated – as special, distinct, and multifaceted individuals. It is about creating honest messaging that speaks specifically to your target customer in a way that feels personalized to them. That doesn't just mean addressing them by first name, it means showing them marketing messages that reflect your knowledge and care for them.

It is the realization that effective digital marketing has changed. The customer is in charge more than ever before. The customer knows integrous marketing when they see it. YOU-centric marketing understands that the customer not only wants transparency and ethics from their products and services, they also want to support brands that represent themselves because people buy identities, namely their own.

The essential point is that you need to treat your target customer as the individual they are. You need to understand them. You need to know what they value and appreciate, as well as what they don't. And you need to treat your target customer with the same respect you would give your neighbor. You would never walk up to your neighbor and just try to sell them something. You would chat about their day, their plans and their life. You would make the conversation about them, not you. The same applies to your marketing. The more your customer feels like your messaging is designed exclusively to communicate with them, the more likely they are to invite you into their inbox, their social feed, and their lives. This access to their lives makes it far more likely that they will ultimately purchase from you. They realize that your company actually cares about them – a rarity in a world ruled by transactional relationships.

Now you might be asking yourself, *How is putting your customer needs first new? Haven't marketers been doing this for years?* Sadly, not really. Traditional marketing has long relied on interruption, which is the opposite of fulfilling your customer's needs. They interrupt your life with television commercials designed to force you to take notice. They interrupt you with billboards on your commute as you gaze at the surrounding scenery. They disrupt you with ads in your feed that you must watch to access the content that you were actually seeking out. This is why the ad agencies of today focus so much of their attention on the creative and the next big campaign idea – the goal being if the disruption is clever, cute, entertaining, etc., then you won't mind the interruption. Nonetheless, it is still a disruption, something you patiently accept because you want to watch your favorite TV show. But that isn't how you build a relationship with your customers. Annoying them into submission may work when someone is ready to buy, but it doesn't work on fostering a relationship or engaging them before they're ready to purchase. Your target customer just employs their highly-honed advertisement blindness technique and moves on with their life (while your brand pays through advertising dollars only to be ignored).

Classic marketing is transactional, whereas YOU-centric marketing is built on the principals of what Seth Godin (best-selling author, entrepreneur and marketing blogger extraordinaire) refers to as Permission Marketing. Permission marketing gains your customer's permission by having them "opt-in" to reading your company's blog, watching your video, downloading your ebook or listening to your podcast. Permission marketing gives the customer something of such value that they will seek it out on their own because it matters to them. YOU-centric takes Permission marketing one step further by making the communication feel personal or customized to an individual's specific needs and wants. It answers the customer's thoughts by saying, *Yes, this is relevant to me.*

YOU-centric marketing earns more than your customers' trust. It says, *I value you. I value you enough to work to earn your business by giving, giving and giving you what you want because you're worth it.* Wouldn't you like to be marketed to in this way?

Chapter 5: **Content Marketing is the New Advertising**

YOU-centric marketing and content marketing is a match made in heaven when used properly. Content Marketing is a buzzword that often gets thrown around by marketers. However, many don't really understand what it means or are not clear on how to effectively apply it to their marketing strategy. Content marketing is used to stimulate interest in your brand by utilizing content that is of interest to your target audience. Think of content describing the best yoga moves for improving strength, brought to you by your favorite active-wear clothing company. Content marketing doesn't explicitly promote your brand. The most straightforward way to think of content marketing is that it speaks to your customer's interests. Content marketing educates you, it informs you. It entertains and delights you. It motivates and inspires you. What do all of these have in common? You. However, content marketing differs from YOU-centric marketing because it is often used to supplement or augment brand-centric content. It isn't a marketing philosophy that prioritizes and consistently delivers hyper-targeted YOU-centric content to your target audience. In fact, most marketers dabble in content marketing by using a little bit of content marketing here and there in an attempt to remind customers that not every piece of content is about the brand. This is where marketers fall short; they assume that if they create content marketing assets that meet their customer's interests and aspirations every once in a while, they can get away with features and benefits content the rest of the time. That doesn't mean that you never highlight the features and benefits of your brand, but rather, the order is reversed; the brand-centric content occasionally augments YOU-centric marketing messaging, not the other way around.

That doesn't mean you should hide your brand in the messaging, but it means your brand takes a back seat. You see, content marketing has nothing to do with what your company sells. Instead it says, *Let's figure out what you care about and provide that type of content to you.* It seeks to offer something of value to your audience. This is why YOU-centric marketing and content marketing is an ideal marriage – because content marketing is rooted in the fundamentals of putting your customer's interests first. However, YOU-centric marketing is the next evolution of content marketing because it moves beyond tactics to an on-going marketing mindset. For instance, the next content example for the aforementioned active-wear customer might be a video on the best weekend-getaway wellness spas in the country because the clothing company understands that their customers value a mind, body, spirit approach to wellness.

The idea behind content marketing is to provide truly helpful, beneficial and/or interesting content to your target audience. To put it simply, giving them something for nothing, but it has to really be of some worth and usefulness. It absolutely, positively cannot be a veiled sales pitch because consumers are keen at seeing through advertisements disguised as content marketing. The important thing to remember (and it often gets forgotten) is that content marketing isn't about your brand, it's about your audience. By providing something that resonates with your audience or is something of interest to them, you are building brand loyalty which will eventually translate into a sale and hopefully many sales. Think of it as the long game that pays dividends in the end.

Another equally important aspect of content marketing is the uniqueness of the content that you are generating. Producing another fluff-filled blog – absent of any new, interesting, or read-worthy information – will be of little value to your target audience. That isn't effective content marketing. However, creating something distinct that really serves the evolving needs and wants of your customers is when content marketing really delivers positive results for your brand. Your brand is then viewed as a trusted resource, partner or friend (yes, friend). One only needs to look at brands like REI or Patagonia to see the reality of this statement. Patagonia is an outstanding example of a company that really understands and utilizes a YOU-centric philosophy with their content marketing. They produce an awe-inspiring magazine with incredible photography that also functions as a product catalog. Within the magazine's pages are unique and interesting stories of outdoor enthusiasts. These stories resonate with a target audience that appreciates the individual experience of an outdoor adventure. They cover trail runners, rock climbing and family adventures that connect personally to the reader. Understanding that their customers are intrigued by areas beyond outdoor recreation, the magazine also includes conservation reports, a "good reads" book review, and healthy recipes. All of which speaks to the deep understanding that Patagonia has about the needs of their customers. They truly understand what motivates and inspires them. At the same time, clothing and gear have been carefully curated and included in the magazine based on their relevance to the content. A great reminder that Patagonia understands that the brand comes second or supplements the YOU-centric content not the other way around.

It was a classic rainy spring day when my client called me to talk about his marketing. Nathan worked for a large multinational brand. He had been with the company for a few years and was trusted and respected. Nathan's concern, and the reason for his call, was that the company had spent so many years focused on sales materials and other brand-first initiatives that he feared his competition was beginning to get a leg up. His competition had begun focusing more on customer needs, and that meant that his company's marketshare could soon be in jeopardy.

After thinking through the best content marketing strategy, we developed a plan to position his company in an exclusive way. As a result, we embarked on creating a YOU-centric series of highly visual (beautiful imagery, layout and design), digestible content that focused on the consumer trends. Importantly, there was no mention of the company's products or any other commercial element outside of a *Learn More* link to their website. Instead, the content focused solely on what mattered to their customers. The brand moved away from their traditional approach of putting their products in the forefront and instead started providing high-value educational content. At the same time, we began a different content marketing series which provided a behind the scenes feel in order to truly connect with their audience.

It wasn't an easy transition because the company was rooted in a commercial approach to their content creation (and they still had that type of information on their website and sales aids, as they should), but they decided to change the way they consistently communicated with customers to make it YOU-centric. As a result, the company's sales leads increased, the sales team became re-engaged because they had unique, informative YOU-centric marketing to share with their best prospects. Nathan also increased the company's investment in on-going content marketing because he experienced the positive outcome firsthand.

What did Nathan really do as a result of shifting to a YOU-centric content marketing strategy? He improved his company's story. He told his company's story in a different, more engaging, thoughtful way, and he set the foundation for future stories to be told. He made the company's story matter to his customers. He consistently answered the consumer's questions, and his customers responded. Nathan realized the power of storytelling and he took full advantage of it. How is your business using storytelling? If the answer is that you aren't or you aren't sure then read on.

Chapter 6: **What's Your Story?**

In the ever-increasing busy life of the average consumer, one thing is for certain; everyone is multitasking nearly all the time. This multitasking happens at work, on the weekends and everywhere in between. It is habitual, and it also impacts their media consumption. Many have their phone in hand as they watch TV with a laptop propped on their lap, just in case a work email comes through. So when it comes to connecting with your target audience, you better put something irresistible in front of them if you want to capture their attention for even a fleeting moment. Enter YOU-centric storytelling.

Unlike traditional features and benefits driven marketing, a story naturally stops you in your tracks. Think of how many times you are in the midst of small talk when someone around you begins telling a story. Suddenly, the room falls to a hush to hear the tale. In this case, it doesn't matter if the story is particularly good, it still grabbed everyone's attention instantly. The same applies to marketing (all but the bad story part). Your brand should be constantly thinking about your story or stories, and how you can best share them with your audience in a YOU-centric way that is meaningful to them.

The best part is that there are so many stories to tell! You can tell the story of how your company was founded. Those early day insights are engaging because you are part of the American dream. You started something from scratch, toiled, worked at it and made mistakes, but ultimately your business grew and prospered. This is a YOU-centric approach because who doesn't relate to that or see themselves aspiring to achieve greater success.

If your company history is a bit on the lackluster side, think of showcasing your employee stories. Every great organization has a few shining stars whose stories are worth sharing. Think of the social media stories about the hardworking young man who walked miles to and from work every morning because he couldn't afford a car, until one day his fellow coworkers bought him one. Sure, you would hope that your employees are making enough to purchase their own car, but the truth is that this person was just starting his career, so a helping hand was needed. Nonetheless, this story was real, raw and authentic. How many of your customers could see themselves or someone they know in this story? How many would say, *That sounds similar to my story and That feels relevant to me?* Storytelling doesn't get more real, approachable or YOU-centric than that.

You can also share your community story. This is the opportunity to shine a spotlight on your tribe or your consumer advocates through user-generated (real people sharing their genuine feedback) content. There are all kinds of creative ways that you can share their stories which will not only breed additional loyalty, but also provide a connection to your community and the people who stand with your brand. Don't get me wrong, this shouldn't be an infomercial using real customers (please, no). This should really be their story. Your brand should not be the focal point. Still, you could create a whole series of customer stories such as young professionals balancing life and work while making a difference in their communities brought to you by a popular retailer, for example. A perfect example of awesome storytelling about a company's customers was P&G's brilliant *Thank you, Mom* Olympic stories. Although these stories weren't real people or user-generated, they had a tremendous impact because they had very real application to their target audience: Moms. Talk about making your customer feel appreciated and important with beautiful YOU-centric execution!

What Mom doesn't want to be recognized and appreciated? I still can't see these commercials without tearing up because it relates to me. Because of these stories, I'm happy to support a brand who understands Moms.

There are more stories to tell too. You can share your company's giving back story, detailing how your company is contributing to the betterment of the planet through various charitable activities. These stories work particularly well with Millennials who wear social consciousness as a badge of honor and want to support brands that represent their values. More than that, these are great stories to tell because it shows what companies can do when it isn't all about the bottom-line and profits. When it's about being part of something bigger than themselves, great things happen. Think of what a well-known, minimalistic shoe company has done to separate their brand by giving away a pair of shoes for every pair sold. What company wouldn't be proud to put themselves in the same light as some of the best known foundations or other charitable powerhouses that remember that with success comes great responsibility? And what customer wouldn't be happy to pay a little more for the product if they too could be part of giving back, especially if giving back or contribution is a core value to them?

There is also your product story. This may be more challenging to make interesting, but it can be done. Marriott's Golden Rule story is a great example of cleverly telling your brand story in a relatable, personal, YOU-centric way that impacts their target audience. Making the connection between treating people the way you want to be treated and the hotel chain's approach to business is a great way to tell their product story without it feeling overly focused on the product. I love that they took the approach of tapping into something that has both broad appeal and historical roots. After all, who doesn't want to stay at a hotel that treats you the way you want to be treated? More than that, this story can have many iterations, which means it provides the best kind story-telling – a story that connects and expands to other stories. Think of it as a series of stories that all fit into the brand's positioning.

The other point about storytelling is that even brands that profess to bypass the whole story thing (think Brandless) are actually utilizing storytelling as well. Brandless' story is that they are too cool to have a story. However, the notion that Brandless is making Generic label hip again is really their story, whether they claim it or not. Consumers who wish to be thought of as being without labels or airs (and there are many of them) love the idea of supporting a brand just like themselves because people buy identities not products. The point is that every brand has a story to tell, you just have to think about which stories are worth sharing and why they matter to your customers. Once you determine that, you are on the path to marketing to people in a way that cuts through the clutter and the noise, because it feels personal to your target customer.

Mike's story illustrates this point. I started working with Mike through a referral. Mike had a vision of creating a lifestyle brand that was deeply connected to his target customer's spiritual health. Mike believed that being truly happy opens up the opportunities for you to focus on other growth areas of your life. The thought process being that when you feel lousy you can't really focus on much else, but when you feel joyful you can focus on contributing to your life and your world in other positive ways. Mike's brilliant storytelling vision was to explicitly connect the brand with personal growth and development.

When I first heard this, I wondered why no one else had made this connection or thought to brand their product in this way. In truth, it is a bit of a risky endeavor because it narrows your target audience to consumers that are on a personal growth path, but the ingenious part of it is that it concentrated the brand's attention on connecting with a tribe of like-minded people, which is really where the power lies. So we went about creating stories that would empower the target audience to live their best lives.

We started with a podcast series, which was a simple Q&A format designed to highlight the growth and advancement in his life. This approach gave us the ability to expand the story(s) to include consumer, influencer and others of a similar ilk, with each one reinforcing the next to keep the story going. We started a personal story that was relevant to people who are also on a spiritual or personal growth.

From there we hired seasoned bloggers to write unique and captivating articles which included spiritual undertones that provided inspiration as well as knowledge. We also incorporated a playful tone because spiritual growth and improving your health is fun, so why not highlight it? We then went about building other informative and motivational content assets that reflected the target audience's needs, interests and aspirations. In short, we made it all about them. You guessed it – we made it YOU-centric.

We used a storytelling approach that focused on their educational health needs in a distinct way, which also offered true support and encouragement. It worked. This allowed us to offer a different experience to customers. It allowed us to separate the brand from an extremely crowded market and chart our own unique course. It also allowed us to use storytelling to create a powerful customer experience. YOU-centric storytelling creates an experience for your customers because it encapsulates your brand's mission, purpose and values into something that is approachable, relevant and real.

The important thing to remember is that your story isn't just added to your website and forgotten. Rather, you have to bring your story to life in different formats (video, memes, blogs, webinars, podcasts) and distribute it across multiple platforms: email marketing, social media, content syndication, advertising, etc. You need to share snippets or aspects of your story, all the time, in your content and marketing creation. This approach allows you to capitalize on your story while maximizing its exposure and keeping it in front of your customers. It also helps you avoid losing your brand identity once the next new idea, trend or campaign is cultivated. It keeps you engaging with your customers in ways that matter to them.

Chapter 7: **How to Tell Your Story**

It all begins with the content assets themselves. When thinking through a YOU-centric content marketing strategy, begin with the elements of the brand that work well for the overarching story and would be of interest and value to your target audience. Some content assets retell and/or reinforce the story, such as a blog, while others explain the story, such as a quick resource guide. Others keep the story going, and still others, such as tutorials, expand the story. It is important to keep all of these aspects in mind when developing your content marketing strategy and, of course, these stories have to be consistently communicated across your brand platforms. You have to have an integrated approach. Simply put, the story needs to integrate with your other stories and be comprehensive. The last thing you want is for your brand to feel schizophrenic when viewed as a whole, and it needs to focus on your target audience. Again, it must be YOU-centric from start to finish.

Blogs

Let's start with the simplest, albeit one of the most creative content assets first: your blog. All businesses – both ecommerce, and products and services – should produce and distribute some form of original YOU-centric content, as opposed to just sharing articles or other people's content, and a blog is the perfect content asset to utilize. Blogs tend to be roughly 500-800 words so they are quick pieces of content to generate. They are highly visual because they include at least one image or photograph, and they are excellent at creating a valuable connection with your audience. Plus, a great blog is enjoyable to read. I absolutely adore reading a popular mom blog, and I make it a priority to read because it is relevant to me. It provides valuable, raw, honest commentary about being a mother. As a mother, I appreciate the candor, but even more than that is the fact that the blog makes me feel like part of a tribe, back to that whole community thing. A blog is a great asset for creating community because of its frequency and the ability to reinforce ideas, passions and purpose.

Your blog should have these same goals. It should be highly pertinent, engaging, and pleasurable to your audience. It should also have a fresh angle or perspective to keep it relevant in the sea of seemingly similar content. You may not want to hear this, but you can't relegate blog writing to your college-aged niece (and seriously, you have no idea how many times I hear that the blog writing function is given to the CEO's cousin's daughter who is all of 18). If your college niece is a phenomenal writer and happens to really understand the needs and wants of your target audience, that is fine, but that rare circumstance is the exception to the rule. Rather, give the blog writing responsibilities to an excellent writer. We recommend using journalists or professional bloggers who truly understand YOU-centric content marketing and understand how to connect and engage with your customers. Blog writing is an important role, and it is well worth the investment to hire someone who is skilled in this regard.

The reason original content is important is that constantly sharing other articles from sources such as magazines and newspapers with your audience gets stale and leaves your brand largely out of the conversation. Juxtaposing this with original content that you produce allows you to craft the conversations that have the most relevance to your audience while reflecting their attitudes and lifestyle ideals. That doesn't mean you shouldn't share interesting articles with your audience too, it is just that it shouldn't be your default mode (and please, never be in default mode).

The other important thing to remember about your blog is that it shouldn't be all about your brand or category. It must be YOU-centric. For example, if you are an organic yogurt company, all of your blogs shouldn't be about yogurt. Sure, you can have some blogs on the best healthy snacks for kids or the grab-and-go quality of yogurt for a summer road trip or something along those lines, but the bulk of your blogs should focus on health, wellness, active lifestyles, and other content that reflects the well-rounded interests of your target audience.

ClifBars realized this early on, and they are one of the best examples of a blog that goes beyond energy bars. Their blogs focus on everything from the individual story of an Ironman athlete, to equal pay for women, to where to catch the best surfing waves. Why? Because they know their audience cares about this type of content. They also know that keeping customers engaged on their website via non-brand specific content is wise because it drives repeat visitation and stickiness (meaning people stay on their site longer). They also understand that content exclusively relating to their product category or brand gets old relatively quickly and isn't very inspiring. Think about it – even the biggest energy bar aficionado doesn't want to read about it all the time.

This type of broader content also hits on affinity interests. ClifBars could have very easily focused on athlete stories or on adventure stories, but instead they also went after policy blogs which spark conversations while associating ClifBar with issues their customers have an affinity with. ClifBars says we care about you and understand you enough to create the content that you care about. This is blog creation at its finest, and it works.

Other brands wrongly assume that the customer is interested only in category or product specific content. For example, I have read blogs generated from a facial toner product company because at one time I was their customer. This company creates blogs, but each one ties back to their product. For instance, they create blogs such as the best products for treating acne, and include a write up of their product within the blog. The next blog talks about really cleansing your skin for optimum health, and has a product write up included, and so on and so on. In fact, every one of their blogs focuses on both their product category and their products themselves. Talk about a one trick pony.

Think of this from the perspective of the consumer. Do you want to read about facial toner in every blog that you read? Even if you are a die-hard health and beauty fanatic, wouldn't you get a bit tired of this content? The answer is a resounding yes. Of course you would because we aren't one dimension beings. We are multifaceted, multi-interest people who like a little variety in our content consumption.

It is one thing to include a link to your products in your blog (that is smart because it drives interested customers to evaluate your products further), but when every blog includes your products, it feels like a sales aid masquerading as a blog. You might be able to fool your audience into reading a bit of this content, but eventually the faux blog becomes of little interest, and your open and engagement rates will suffer. The same applies to writing about your category exclusively instead of the lifestyle that your brand represents and, more importantly, your customer's interests. It is also a rather lackadaisical approach to blog writing which should be engaging, unique and of real value in fulfilling your customer's wants and needs. It should be YOU-centric.

Ebooks

Now let's take a peek at ebooks. While they may sound like a daunting content asset to create, they are, in reality, far easier to produce than perceived. The beauty of ebooks (we aren't talking about electronic readers here, we are referring to mini-books that your brand creates that can be promoted and downloaded online) is that they can be virtually any size. You can create a four-page ebook or a twenty page ebook. Albeit, we don't encourage twenty page ebooks unless you have technology or research that requires this. Typically, ebooks are short in length, informative, well-designed books that provide education or address a specific need like a '10 Ways to Destress Daily' book. Ebooks are PDFs that can be downloaded from your site and printed. They generally don't require special technology to access, although you can go that route if you desire. Our recommendation is to go with a nicely branded and designed ebook that people can easily download as a PDF and save or print from your site.

Ebooks can focus on a variety of content. You can create new content that focuses on the latest trends in your market, relevant statistics or emerging information. You can use ebooks as a compilation of tips or a guide. Some examples are, 'The Top 20 Foods to Avoid to Tackle Inflammation' or 'The Top 5 Home Security Tips.' The idea being that you can take just about any content and turn it into an ebook as long as it is interesting and meets your customer's needs.

Ebooks can also be a repository of repurposed content. For instance, you could do an ebook on your highest performing blogs (especially if the blogs are evergreen – content that isn't date specific). Ebooks are also ideal for how-tos or tutorial content such as '10 Daily Steps to Improve Your Memory'. They're great for compiling or aggregating your favorite recipes in a certain segment such as 'Keto-Friendly Breakfasts' or 'Fast, Healthy Foods Your Children Will Love.' The possibilities are endless.

The best part is that ebooks feel worth the opt-in. Meaning, you are willing to share your first name, last name, and email address to download an ebook because it feels substantive and worthwhile. As a result, they're the perfect content asset for growing your subscribers lists. They're also the gift that keeps on giving because they can be referred to or reused often (think recipe ebook) which offers strong branding for your business.

Recently, I was chatting with a friend. He mentioned that he was looking for ways to expand his veterinary services while providing greater value. As a new puppy owner (we have a precious English Yellow Lab), I thought through all of the questions that I've had when visiting the vet that I never seemed to get answered. As a result, we talked about creating a series of ebooks that he could offer to educate people on the top 12 things to expect when getting a puppy, their nutrition and health needs, etc. We also discussed that he could do this as a series based on the varying ages and stages of a dog's life. This type of content would be so valuable to me that I mentioned he could charge for it. I would gladly pay to have a trusted source of information educate me on what my dog needs, especially if it comes to me in a convenient format like ebooks where I can simply download and save or print from my computer.

The other benefit to creating ebooks is that it positions your brand as an expert on the subject matter (another win for your company). There are many benefits to creating ebooks, and when they are truly valuable you can charge for them, provide a needed service, and increase your revenues at the same time. Now doesn't that sound like compelling YOU-centric marketing?

Quizzes

I have to admit that I'm in love with quizzes right now. They are amusing, interesting and insightful all at the same time (or at least when they're done well). They're also a great tool for creating customized or personalized YOU-centric content. Is there any wonder that social media is awash with the latest personalized quiz? Who hasn't taken a personality test on Facebook? And who among us hasn't been sucked into trying a new online quiz that seemed intriguing?

The best way to create an awesome quiz is to look at your business and see how you can direct your customers to the right product or service for them based on their quiz answers. Think of it as a personalized quiz that helps them make the right buying decision. For instance, a personal care company may use a quiz to determine if the potential customer has sensitive, dry, oily, or normal skin. By creating the quiz with some if/then scenarios, you can direct your customers to the exact product they need, as well as give them useful tips and education. You should always customize the quiz such that your prospective client receives a detailed or personalized report as a result of taking the quiz. Remember, YOU-centric says that your marketing needs to be all about your customer. Quizzes are an excellent content asset for doing just that. For the aforementioned example, Brett (your potential customer) receives a customized report sent to his inbox which walks him through the best lotion for his dry, cracking skin and what ingredients are important to protect his skin from the weather and ailments, along with a product recommendation or two. In this case, the product(s) recommendations don't come off as salesy but rather the company is doing your research for you, as well as providing a valuable service. This is YOU-centric marketing and content marketing at its best.

In addition to providing great tailor-made content, quizzes also afford an excellent lead generation opportunity because customers are willing to opt-in with their name and email address to get this type of customized content. The value makes it worth the opt-in. Even better, the customer gains an appreciation for the brand that took the time to understand their individual needs instead of putting all of its products in front of them without personalizing the experience.

Quizzes can also push a customer to convert because you have taken the guesswork out of the product selection for them. Don't you love it when you receive a specific recommendation that is just for you? So does your target customer.

Webinars

If your product or service requires education to understand, and many products and services do, then webinars are a great content asset to create for your business. It has never been easier to host a webinar. You can use a service which provides video conferencing at an inexpensive rate.

Webinars are also great for showcasing the experts within your business or bringing in well-known panelists to provide credence and additional allure for your target audience. Webinars are a great YOU-centric asset because many potential customers want to learn more or increase their knowledge, and webinars answer this call. While webinars sound complicated to create, a strong educational focus, a presentation, some visuals, and an engaging speaker is all that is really required.

In addition, you can chunk your webinar content into digestible segments and run them as an educational series. Personal growth companies are experts at doing this. They take a concept like creating the life you want while focusing each webinar on a section of that greater goal. For instance, the first webinar might be on goal setting, the second might focus on visualization, and the final might focus on daily affirmations that you use to help energize reaching your goals. The topics are different, but they all fit into the overall content umbrella of improving your life. The beauty of this approach is that the commitment feels more manageable because you can attend one, two or all three, depending on your specific needs.

As with other content assets, webinars are excellent for lead generation because your target customer tends to be more than willing to hand over their contact information because webinars have a high-level of perceived value. They're viewed as being of significance or worth, and rightfully so! This assumes you are hosting free webinars, but you could also structure them as a paid online course that offers high-level learning.

Paid webinars are great for companies that know they have educational information of great worth to share (this is particularly true for learning curriculums) because your customers will pay for really exceptional content. Plus, they give participants the convenience of learning on their own time and in the comfort of their home or office. This is YOU-centric because it puts the needs of your customers first. They also provide passive and/or ancillary income for your business because they can be archived and promoted repeatedly so the upfront time and expense are recouped exponentially. How is that for a true YOU-centric win-win?

Videos

Video is all the rage, and if you aren't using it for your business, you should be. It is naturally engaging, and it is becoming increasingly easier to produce since shooting video on your phone and distributing it to the masses has become perfectly acceptable. Of course, this doesn't work for all brands, but most brands could use a little of the behind-the-scenes genuineness that cell phone videos bring to the table. However, that doesn't mean that any content is worthy of a video. Your video needs to tell a story that is truly worth your customer's time. It also needs to answer the question, *Why should I care?* Immediately.

Video is the perfect avenue for YOU-centric storytelling. After all, storytelling is why film was invented to begin with. Video allows you to create a narrative around your product, lifestyle or aspirations, just like a good movie. You start by introducing the characters and the setting, and you set into motion the sequence of events such as a problem or conflict that you are trying to solve. As the video proceeds, your characters and settings grow or change as does the plot in response to the circumstances. Ultimately, this leads to the climax of the story. The climax is the event the plot builds to which offers insight and ultimately a resolution or solution to the problem. While this may seem abstract, a narrative arch is the basis for all compelling video, and it absolutely applies to the stories you want to tell with your brand.

Beyond that, video can breathe life into an otherwise mundane product. Think of using video to describe the biggest challenges facing your customer. The mattress company Purple offers great insight into taking products that are not flashy in the least and making them interesting, with great video tutorials that show the problem and the solution. For instance, mattresses are not the sexiest product to sell; and it is an increasingly crowded category. However, Purple shows the construction of the mattress and the employees that work on them in an artistic, albeit campy way that makes it interesting. The same applies to your business. What separates your product or service from the competition? Use whatever this is and make an interesting video that conveys how your product improves the customer's life while making it about your customer.

Another excellent opportunity that video affords is the chance to create an original series. While the creation of an original series tends to come with some considerable cost, there are ways to minimize the expenses such as shooting multiple episodes over a few days, as well as creating or editing into short (roughly 15 minute) videos, having a small video crew (just a few people), and taking advantage of a natural setting (versus a studio that comes at an additional cost). An awesome example of a brand doing this right, and YOU-centric, is YETI. Recently while on a flight, I stumbled upon an original series presented by YETI. The series explored a professional fly-fishing guide as he floated on the river, fished and genuinely examined personal aspects of his life and work. Although I'm not a fisherwoman, I got completely sucked into the episode, and if there is one thing that YETI knows, outside of outstanding marketing, it is their customer's wants, desires, needs and aspirations. I can just imagine the joy of a fisherman watching this episode. It would feel uniquely curated just for him or her. That is why the episode on the low-key fishing guide was so powerful. It was YOU-centric from start to finish, it connected with their target audience about something that they care about – the outdoors, the personal connection to nature, and of course, fishing. It also was delivered in a minimalist yet compelling reality format that showed a real person, with authentic emotions, doing what he loves. What fisherman doesn't relate to that?

The other piece that I greatly admire is that YETI didn't cheapen the experience with product placements, shots of the YETI logo throughout or anything else brand-centric in the series. Instead, the series used storytelling to connect with their audience in a way that is true to their interest. It wasn't forced or gimmicky, it was just great content. At the end of the short series, the YETI logo flashed with a "presented by" and that was the extent of the brand promotion. This thoughtful approach gave YETI the opportunity to connect with its audience and separate themselves from other brands that are all about themselves. This is a great example of a brand who truly understands YOU-centric marketing.

Video gives a more personal view of who your company is and what makes your brand unique. If you apply this thinking to your video, remembering that it isn't about you but rather about solving, improving, uplifting, motivating, and/or meeting your customer's needs, you will undoubtedly produce a successful YOU-centric video.

Resource Guides

This type of content asset can be just about anything. A great YOU-centric resource guide could be something like a list of the best toxic-free home cleaning products. Resource guides can also be used to compare similar products and different features, benefits or functions, e.g., a list of the differences between TV brands. This is an excellent content asset for reaching potential customers farther down the buying funnel (people who are closer to making a purchase), who are looking to evaluate or compare your product to other products (they want additional assurance before becoming a customer).

Moreover, this type of content is hugely useful because it tends to be informative one-sheets that meet a specific customer need, desire or want. Often, sales aids have this type of comparative information, and this is an ideal way to repurpose this information and share it with a new audience. The great news is that you don't have to reinvent the wheel, you just need to look at some of your content and see what would serve as a helpful guide, add some design elements (again, you want this to be beautiful and profession-ally done), and you're off to the races with creating YOU-centric resource guides.

Contests

If you are active on social media, you have undoubtedly been exposed to a contest. Social media is the ideal outlet for contests because they drive engagement and traffic to your site. They are also easy to participate in and offer the incentive or reward of winning a prize, so it's no wonder they work well. I know some people think of contests as just another low quality or largely irrelevant traffic driver to your site, and that can certainly happen, depending on the structure, target audience, objectives and make-up of your contest, but they can also be hugely beneficial. Like all things, it depends on the contest itself.

I recommend thinking and going big with your YOU-centric contest. If you are going to put all the effort into creating a contest, and even if you use an app like Gleam, there is still much work in the rules and coordination, so you might as well make the payoff worth the effort. Think of your contest as an extension of your brand experience and go big! Offer a unique trip or experience (concert tickets, wine tasting, bike tour) for two, along with a few months' supply of your product and free merchandise or gift bag.

It is better to do fewer contests that are substantial rather than multiple smaller contests. You get a much bigger bang for your buck when there is an allure and urgency to the contest because it is both significant and infrequent. I know many brands like to do several small contests to drive traffic, but that dilutes the importance and makes it less likely that you will reach the right consumer who is actually interested in your products or services. Larger contests, in contrast, tend to offer more promotional build up, exposure, reach and excitement.

The other important element of a successful contest is to do it with integrity. I once worked with a brand that would offer a contest which included several months of free services. They used the contest to drum up excitement and planned to select the winner at one of their upcoming events. I thought this a great way of combining online and offline efforts until I learned that they had no intention of giving away the services. Rather, they planned to "select" someone who wasn't present at the event (you had to be present to win) because they didn't really want to give away their services. Of course, my company immediately walked away from the contest idea with this client because it lacked integrity, and we don't play that. Anything that is less than on the up-and-up will come back to bite you. Rigging a contest is really penny wise and pound foolish because although you will likely get away with it, if you do this enough, you will get caught and your brand's reputation will be ruined. Even if you don't get caught, consumers have an uncanny way of sensing when a company is not being honest. If you don't really want to offer a great contest, just don't do a contest, do something else of value. It is far better to develop another traffic and engagement tactic than to sell off your integrity.

Creating unique content assets help in telling or reinforcing stories that you want associated with your brand. They reinforce your commitment to YOU-centric marketing because they are designed to meet a specific need, interest, lifestyle or aspiration. They're also ideal for promoting on social media, your website, email marketing, and other avenues because they require very little commitment from your target audience outside of their time and an opt-in. That means they provide value as well as a low barrier to entry, such that you can connect and engage with new potential customers to your brand. As such, the time commitment becomes far less important and the value becomes paramount. Look at your business and see what content can be turned into something else. Don't be afraid to repurpose or reuse. Concentrate on the benefit to your customer. Ask yourself, What would be the biggest benefit to my audience? What assets do I have or can I create that will contribute to their knowledge and meet their needs? How can I be of service? How can I give them what they really need? When you can answer these questions and feel excited about what you are giving, you have found the right content asset for your audience.

Once you have the answers, create a powerful YOU-centric contest and share it with your target audience. Share it with the intention of helping them in some way (even if it is just to bring your target audience more joy) and see the results.

Chapter 8: **Quality Over Quantity**

Another aspect of the YOU-centric approach to marketing is that it focuses on giving customers exactly what they need and want, not wasting their time. That means your brand's focus needs to be on producing high quality content and a unique experience. Put another way, the emphasis should be placed on quality over quantity. What customer wants to be exposed to a plethora of low quality content? More than that, doing so devalues your relationship with your target audience because it places your business needs over their needs which is the opposite of YOU-centric.

Recently, I was attending a marketing conference in San Diego (I'm all about continual learning) and the presenter mentioned that his clients create and publish new content daily. At first, I thought I had misheard him, but later he referenced it again. While it is clear that this strategy was working for his clients, the truth is that even the most prolific authors of this world would have difficulty producing great content at this clip. So let me be clear: there is no value in creating content for content's sake. An ocean of poor quality or hastily produced content will do very little outside of drowning your writers. Think of it this way – you don't want to be perceived as the cheap tabloid of brands.

The truth is that crafting interesting, distinct and relevant YOU-centric content takes time. It isn't something that can be rushed with an exclusive focus on driving traffic to your site. You may drive traffic, but low quality content can do more harm than good. How many times have you clicked on a blog or article only to read it and think that you wanted your five minutes back? That experience is the antithesis of YOU-centric marketing. I have had that experience enough times that I now make a note of the sites that may be great at writing an interesting headline but lacks any substance or thought in their writing. It is the old adage – fool me once, shame on you, fool me twice, shame on me. I won't be tricked into coming back to your site for garbage content, and I don't feel particularly good about the brand that engages in such activities. Guess what? Neither does your target audience.

The other challenge with pushing out large quantities of poorly written content is that you tend to attract the wrong audience. Your target audience appreciates a certain level of content. If you dumb it down or change the focus in order to make it easier to produce more of it, you are likely securing traffic from someone who isn't actually your target audience and/or has little interest in what you sell. That doesn't mean expanding your content to reach new audiences shouldn't be done, but it means that your highest goal is to secure qualified traffic, even if it means less overall traffic. In essence, low quality traffic does little for you in the way of conversions so don't get swayed by traffic numbers alone.

Instead, create quality content that your audience wants to read. Think of the trends or latest happenings in your market. These veins are often rich with ideas that are just waiting to be uncovered and written about. Look at other industries and see what type of content they are creating that might have some application or twist that could make it interesting to yours. Examine the frequently asked questions that your customers have and see if you can create a great content asset out of them. Review the problems that your product or service solves and see if there are ancillary topics that also assist in addressing your customer's needs and wants. There are endless possibilities when you stop and think about it, and all of these convey the YOU-centric approach of honoring your target audience by giving them something of true interest to them.

The next step is to create an integrated content calendar. This doesn't have to be fancy, but you should write out the topics that you plan to write about and the format; e.g., blog, ebook, video, etc. Then take this one step further and see if the content marries with any of the other seasonal or monthly happenings. For instance, the months leading up to summer might be the perfect time to create an exercise video for getting swimsuit ready. Moreover, you can tie your content into industry events or trade shows such as The Top 5 Business Growth Trends. These content assets can prove to be helpful resources that also capture the attention of people who are attending the event. The same can be said for upcoming holidays. Think of a gift guide for Dad in advance of Father's Day. This approach makes your content timely as well as relevant, and conveys that you understand your audience has more on their mind than just your brand.

A well-crafted content calendar will also give you an opportunity to look at the resources needed to execute – and not just execute, but execute well. We often start by recommending that brands start with approximately four blogs per month. Why? Because this is a reasonable amount of content to produce in a month, and blogs should be repeatedly promoted because very few people read the blog when it is first published. This means that a single blog can be promoted multiple times without feeling stale. This also affords the opportunity and time required to bring in pertinent research and trends, as well as other interesting tidbits into your blogs.

From there we expand the content creation into things like short tutorial videos, webinars and other high-value content assets. This allows you to promote new and different things to your audience, while getting you out of a single format focus. In addition, this is an excellent time to look at past content that could be refreshed or repurposed. There is no need to reinvent the wheel; use what you have but update it or apply it to another format.

Utilizing these tactics will make content creation much more manageable while giving you an opportunity to look at your content calendar with a critical eye. You should ask, *Is this content really useful to my target audience? Is this content pertinent based on what else is happening during this time of year? Is there content that I'm missing or opportunities to engage my customers with something new?* It all starts with preparing a calendar and once completed, sharing the calendar with your team such that the content isn't siloed (only shared with select members of your marketing team) or isolated to one department or group. Instead, it is being reinforced via email marketing, social media, website, advertising, and other ways. You get the picture. Once you have it outlined, you can use it to foster an integrated marketing approach that is holistic. Once you perfect that approach, that is when your content creation really pays off because it increases your target audience's affinity for your brand.

Chapter 9: **The Ever-Changing Customer**

Perhaps nowhere has the disruption in marketing been more pronounced than with the customer. Today's consumer is literally bombarded by brand messages. It is estimated that consumers see and hear 10,000 brand messages per day. That is a lot of messages! No wonder consumers suffer from advertising blindness. That is just too much features and benefits content to take in.

Perhaps because of feeling overwhelmed with messaging, consumers have high expectations in terms of understanding your brand quickly or, to be more precise, they need to understand it immediately. In fact, the average visitor to your site consumes your content for fifteen seconds or less, and that statistic is from a few years ago. The number today is probably closer to ten seconds. That means your brand messaging needs to be succinct, distinct and interesting to your target audience all at the same time. Simply put, your potential customers need to get your unique selling proposition at first glance. You would be amazed at the number of times we are working with a client that thinks their brand messaging is crystal clear only to be shocked when we say, "We don't get it," and my team reads the content for longer than fifteen minutes, as opposed to a mere fifteen seconds! This is why taglines are used so often; they distill the most important aspects of the brand in a quick few words or sentences. The sad fact is that your customers no longer read. They aren't going to look through several paragraphs of your website to understand your products, services or advantages. They aren't going to read past a sentence or two into your blog, so make your messaging clear, concise, engaging and easy (and I mean really easy) to understand. They need to see the relevance to them right away.

The other change in consumer behavior is that today's consumers have exceedingly high expectations when it comes to the ease of working with you. When you think of your site in terms of the customer, you need to ask the questions: *How easy is it to find what customers are seeking? How intuitive is the navigation? How easy is the check-out process; multiple steps or very few?* These issues become even bigger with mobile users who aren't apt to click through multiple pages while shopping on their phone. It is crucial that you make it easy for your customers to find what they need. Simply put, even your website design, navigation and user experience needs to be YOU-centric.

It is equally important that you keep the consumer's intent front and center. *What is the intent of your visitors? Is he/she comparative shopping and in need of some product reviews or testimonials to push them over the top? Are they ready to purchase but just want the best deal where a pop-up coupon might do the trick or are they completely sold on your product and just need an easy and seamless check-out process?* These elements matter if you hope to avoid friction (people bouncing out of your site prior to purchasing because they don't think you have what they need or they're confused by the inconsistencies) and the disappointment that follows when you see traffic coming to your site but few conversions.

Consumers also expect greater rewards for their purchases. Gone are the days when free shipping was a big deal. A very large ecommerce brand has made it so that free shipping is almost expected, as is prompt delivery. If you think offering free shipping will push your customers to convert, think again. Say what you will about the aforementioned ecommerce giant, it was sheer ingenuity that they made free shipping with, or even without, their membership and prompt delivery synonymous with their brand. Talk about understanding their customer. When this first launched with these offerings, it was almost unheard of, but it tapped into something that they knew their customers deeply cared about; namely certainty as well as reliability (yes the package will arrive tomorrow), value (free shipping), and the ultimate in convenience. Like it or not, today's customers expect free trials, discounts, giveaways and any other low-barrier to entry offering that makes it easy for them to say yes. This means you need to get more strategic about what you offer and when you offer it. It also means your giveaway had better be really compelling because customers won't take the time to enter if they don't see the value. Customers want to feel rewarded for their efforts beyond discounts or giveaways too. That is one of the reasons why referral marketing is so popular.

Referral marketing gives rewards, namely in discounts, to customers who refer friends to their products or services. This is ingenious because it rewards your best customers while reaching new customers without the heavy customer acquisition cost. It also turns your customers into brand advocates, which is equally brilliant. We delve into this deeper in future chapters, but suffice it to say, we are fans of referral marketing.

Finally, customers now want to feel like they're part of a community. That is another aspect of YOU-centric marketing; customers want to feel like they belong, like they are part of your tribe. This means the more time you spend creating community with your words and actions, the more customers will flock to be part of your clan. It makes sense, doesn't it? Being loyal to a brand is one thing, but being part of a community of like-minded people, well, that is special.

On top of all of this, today's customer also has an acute focus on their own individuality, and they seek products that speak to their uniqueness. Think of it as being akin to the "selfie" culture. The reality is that more consumers are interested in expressing their originality, and they want to purchase from brands that understand that. They want brand messaging that feels customized to meet their distinct peculiarity or uniqueness.

With all the disruptions and evolving originality of the customer, there are a few things that haven't changed. Specifically, the fact that consumers buy identities and emotions. They buy items that reinforce the feelings that are the most important to them. Emotions are the ultimate driver of consumers purchasing decisions. There are six distinct emotions that drive consumer behavior. Some customers crave certainty, reliability and consistency such as the previously mentioned ecommerce customer. They don't want any surprises, they want dependability. Other customers need variety. They need a little spice in their life, a little of the unknown. This might come in the form of an adventure through travel or in purchasing items that feel different or unique. Some customers seek love and connection above all else. They are the people that want to be part of a community, family or something bigger than themselves, while others make purchases to feel significant. This need for significance tends to drive luxury or high-ticket purchases, like vacation homes or luxury automobile purchases. There are customers that buy based on a need for growth or advancement. They seek out items that expand their knowledge or provide a higher level of understanding. Still others purchase based on wanting to contribute. This could be in the form of charity contributions or in purchasing items that have a social cause associated.

The important thing to understand is which of these six emotions are driving your customers. Thoughtfully develop products or services that speak to your target customer's emotional needs. Doing so will mean that you have mastered yet another step of YOU-centric marketing.

Chapter 10: **There is More to Effective Social Media Than Meets the Eye**

Okay, time for a little truth. No one wants to follow a brand on social media. Painful, I realize. To put this statement a better way, no one wants to follow a brand that is all about themselves on social media. Many brands have huge follower numbers (some pay for those bots or faux followers so we don't count them) so how do they do it? Great brands managed to have not only heaps of true followers, but actually engaged followers that readily read, watch and participate with their content (which is far more important than followers for followers sake). You guessed it – the brands that are successful at this, and there are actually many less than you would think, have figured out that their social media page must do two very important things. First, it must convey, restate, and reinforce their unique point of view, which also matches their audience's interests. Second, they give their audience a clear reason why they have this point of view and why they are sharing that point of view. In short, they have a strategy which explains the brand's social media purpose and what that means to you, the consumer. They make their social media presence and communication relevant to you.

They do this by carefully crafting a social media strategy that is larger than themselves and is completely focused on a YOU-centric approach. They think high-level in terms of what will be posted and why, but they also push their limits and move beyond the ordinary. A great place to start is with your company mission. Your company's mission statement tends to be bold, unique, and not specifically aligned to the products that you sell. As a result, it is great fuel for building your strategy. Let's take Nike's mission statement as an example. Nike's mission statement reads: "To bring inspiration and innovation to every athlete* (they define athlete in broad terms) in the world." Guess what? Their social media pages are all about athletes and recreational athletes inspiring people. Their posts tell you why they are posting (to provide inspiration) and their unique point of view; inspiration through innovation. They don't deviate from this mission, and it works.

Another part of developing a successful social media strategy is that it must be consistent with the brand voice. If not, it feels inauthentic or contrived. There is nothing worse than a lack of authenticity on social media. Brands that try to position themselves differently from what they are known to be come off as contrived and disingenuous. Being authentic on social media isn't difficult, but it does take some thought. Start by focusing on your brand's voice then ask some questions. What do you want people on social media to feel in relationship to your brand? Do you want to delight them with fun, entertaining content? Do you want to inform or educate? How do you want your brand to be perceived, and is it consistent with your brand's positioning?

I always start with the overarching purpose of the brand and define it with one word. Focusing on a single word such as "educate", "engage," "amplify" or "delight" is your North Star when it comes to developing your brand voice. Once you have identified the appropriate voice and purpose, look at all of your social media content through this viewpoint; e.g., is this image engaging? Does this video educate? Answering these questions helps you determine if your brand is utilizing YOU-centric marketing that is of interest to your potential customers. If you can connect your posts to your overarching purpose and brand voice, it is easier to stay consistent with your strategy. The last thing you want is off-brand posts that look like your social media manager was out on vacation so you gave the responsibilities to your intern. By the way – of your social media manager is out on vacation, don't give the responsibilities to your intern!

The next step in building your social media strategy is to think of the personality that you wish to convey. Do you want to interact with your audience in a playful manner or in an authoritative manner? It will depend on your type of business. A healthcare provider would likely go with more of an authoritative or expert and informative communication style whereas a fashion business may opt for playful. Again, make your personality reliable and something that your audience has come to expect from your brand. That doesn't mean you can't inject a little humor from time to time, but add levity only if it fits with your strategy.

Once you get the fundamentals of your strategy down, it is time to think of the tactical execution of your strategy. How will you utilize social media to bring traffic to your site or sell your product? Remember, social media is best used for top of funnel or brand awareness (at this stage you are just trying to introduce people or remind people about your brand) and brand loyalty. However, with time and effort, it can turn into another sales channel. With that said, many companies view social media as a sales channel exclusively or primarily. This is why you see so many product shots and offers on social media. The brand's social media feed is essentially: Here is our box of tea next to a cup, here it is next to a bike, here it is with a cookie, here it is in a woman's hand. I can't think of a more dull or uninspiring social media strategy than constant product shots or company updates, and yet you see this all the time. Let me be clear; this is not showcasing your why or what makes you unique, rather, this is a incognito sales pitch. These shots often have captions such as "Buy our latest new tea" or "Click now to get 15% off," and while there is nothing wrong with selling on social media, it should be done strategically. Selling should be a percentage of what you do on social media, along with networking, influencing, and fostering two-way dialogue, but it should not take up the majority of your posts or even 30% of your posts. Because it totally disregards why people are on social media to begin with, and this approach is not customer-centric, it is company-centric.

Beyond that, constantly selling will ultimately result in lower engagement rates and less followers. Nobody goes to social media to be sold to. That doesn't mean you shouldn't showcase your product in interesting environments or interesting formats, just don't over-do it. Your customers have many interests, and repeatedly seeing your product next to an umbrella, in the snow or on the beach probably isn't on the top of your target audience's must-see lists. Some brands can get away with this because they put a lot of time, money and professional photographer's effort into incredibly humorous or delightful images, along with their product shot, but this approach only works for so long.

It is important to remember that being great on social media takes work. However, for some reason, the effort part of the equation tends to get minimized. We see this all the time. Numerous articles claim that social media is easy to get right. Often brands think they can bring a junior level employee (at a low cost) in to implement the social media strategy. They incorrectly think the employee can simply search and find articles to share with their target customer, create an infographic here and there, throw in an occasional meme, and they are off to the races. This is a misperception of epic proportion. The truth is, this approach has failure written all over it. You cannot put forth minimum time, effort and resources into building your social media strategy, so why should you be able to put even less time into executing it? You can't. A thoughtful social media strategy requires pensive implementation, as well as a willingness to examine the execution with fresh eyes and consistently looking for areas of improvement. This is not entry level stuff. If you want to play in social media, make a commitment to it. Invest in your marketing strategy and/or get a team of experts to implement your strategy and pay what it is worth to your brand; namely brand recognition that keeps you top of mind with your customers in a distinct and interesting way which helps maintain existing loyal customers while creating new customers.

The final aspect of developing a winning social media strategy is to treat the platforms differently. That doesn't mean your brand feels different or disjointed from network to network, it means your brand understands the differences of the networks, the demographics and the environment, and respects these differences by utilizing native marketing.

Chapter 11: **Native Marketing**

What is native marketing, you ask? Native marketing is branded content that is intended to promote the brand, but it matches the look and feel of the network or platform. For instance, a Twitter tweet posted on Facebook doesn't resemble the Facebook platform. It resembles Twitter's. To put it more simply, native marketing fits the social media network. Meaning, an Instagram post looks, feels and acts differently than a Facebook post. This is important because Instagram's demographics, platform expectations, characteristics and even its functionality are different than Facebook's. As such, your marketing must reflect the native environment in order to be successful because a Facebook user is different than an Instagram user.

Everyone should understand that even though Facebook owns Instagram, the two networks are fundamentally different. While brands undoubtedly know this, it is amazing how often we see brands posting the exact same social media content on both social networks. Sure, some brands that do this don't want to appear to be "mailing it in," so they post the same exact content on both Instagram and Facebook on different days. While this is, perhaps, a bit more clever, we still aren't fooled.

Why is posting the same content on both networks a problem? Outside of the fact that posting the same content on multiple networks is both boring (and you never want to be dull on social media) and lackadaisical, it also devalues the uniqueness of the social networks and their respective audiences. Instagram isn't Facebook. It's Instagram. It is all about the artistry of the visuals. It is showing your brand's creativity and personality. Instagram offers brands a chance to truly elevate their brand with images and engaging content that separates them from the competition. It affords the opportunity to present your product, the lifestyle it represents, and your target customer's wants and aspirations beautifully. Why would a brand waste a joyous opportunity to engross and connect with potential customers by reposting the same images and content from Facebook on Instagram. We know that Instagram makes it easy to repost on Facebook, but that doesn't mean it is the right social media strategy.

The other distinctive characteristic of Instagram is the page layout. Instagram allows you to create a virtual brand collage because the user sees the entire page when viewing your profile, not just a single image. So in essence, your business's profile page should be thought of as a YOU-centric canvas: the imagery, content, symmetry, and white space should work collectively together. For instance, take a peek at Think's Instagram page as an example: www.instagram.com/thinkmediaconsulting. We don't want to toot our own horn, but our page is attractive as a whole, as well as by single image. Of equal importance, our Facebook page doesn't look like an exact replica of our Instagram page. Sure, it's on brand, but it reflects the uniqueness of Facebook.

The other interesting aspect of Instagram is that this network truly allows you to emphasize your brand's personality, which helps you connect with your target customer in a more personal and friendly way. Your brand can convey its personality not just in the caption of an image or video, but also in the bio itself. More and more brands are using emojis and other fun elements to create lively bios that instill an immediate impression for their brand while encouraging connections with their audience. This is a refreshing inclusion to the more ordinary aspect of stating the who, what and why of your brand. This is another instance of Instagram's and Facebook's differences. Instagram allows brands to be far more playful, whereas Facebook still has a "just the facts" approach to sharing your company overview, mission, and other aspects of your brand.

Another idiosyncrasy of Instagram is the ability to use Instagram Highlights, which means that brands can call to attention the most interesting elements of their company. This is principally the elevator pitch for the brand, but Instagram has raised the bar by making it interesting and fun. More than that, while Facebook recently launched Facebook Stories, it's not the same thing as Highlights so it is worth noting when pointing out the dissimilarities.

All of this is not to say that Instagram is better than Facebook. We love you too, Facebook! It is our love for both networks that compels us to remind brands to treat these amazing social media, and the users of each, networks differently. These are individual, unique platforms, not just another place to post the same content. If you ignore this advice, your brand conveys the impression that it doesn't really care about creating special communities with your target audience on social media. Instead, your social media team is implicitly telling its followers that your brand is just checking off a "to do" instead of valuing the uniqueness of each social network. Be true to Facebook, be true to Instagram, be true to Pinterest, be true to Twitter, be true to SnapChat, and be true to the different customer interactions on each. This is a YOU-centric approach that expands equally, and applies to your target audience and the platform. Be true to the platform, and by treating them differently, you'll end up being true to your followers as well (which is the most important thing!).

Chapter 12: **Instagram**

Determining the right strategy per platform or network takes some effort, but the easiest way to do it is to truly understand the social media network. Once you understand the ways that people interact with a given network, then you can go about creating a strategy that builds on those strengths and connects with your target audience on each platform.

When building out your strategy, make sure you take advantage of specific methods that are native to the platform which maximize your return. Return can be measured by increased follower counts, increased engagement and reach, as well as driving traffic to your site and creating conversions. We always concentrate on the latter because they have the biggest impact on your business, but increasing your follower count with the relevant audience is important to reach your target audience as well. While it is true that follower count is a vanity metric, it is equally true that increasing your follower count also equates to larger reach and improved brand perception. The best way to improve your performance on Instagram is to create a YOU-centric approach and take advantage of the following tactics.

#Hashtags

One of the best ways to improve traffic to your site is to share interesting, desirable and relevant content that your audience wants to engage with, such as blogs, videos, etc. (essentially, all of the content marketing assets outlined in the previous chapter). The next step is to increase the visibility of your posts by using a combination of popular (1M +), moderate (less than 500K), and niche or highly relevant hashtags (100K or less) which speak to or connect with your target audience, such that they're either following these hashtags or searching these hashtags. Hashtags are used to increase your follower count and Likes by categorizing your posts in Instagram for search purposes.

The element that often gets lost when utilizing hashtags on Instagram is the hashtag's relevancy. For instance, you might have a connotation that #shiftinggears means changing course or direction with your life. In an interest to connect with an audience to do just that, you begin using this hashtag throughout your posts; however, a close review of this hashtag reflects that the posts actually have more to do with car gears or equipment and motorcycles. If you're hoping to connect with car enthusiasts, you have the right hashtag, but if you are hoping for a weight loss audience, you have missed the mark. Even professed social media companies use hashtags with little relevance to their customer target because they forget this important step. You must vet your hashtag prior to using it. The good news is that it is easy to do by simply typing the hashtag on Instagram and then clicking through to see the posts and the companies or individuals that are utilizing the tag.

The best bet is to research 20 to 30 hashtags that appear to have the greatest relevance to your target audience then make a list of the hashtags that are, in fact, relevant and YOU-centric. In this example, you may find that ten or so are relevant and the rest are not (unless you are really good at picking potential hashtags). Repeat this exercise again until you have roughly twenty pertinent hashtags that you will include in relevant posts moving forward. Think of this group of hashtags as your everyday hashtags or target audience hashtags, such as #trailrunninglife or #trailrunners if you are looking to connect with a like-minded audience.

When working with clients, we always recommend creating buckets of hashtags then creating a list of ten to twenty hashtags per bucket. The first bucket should include hashtags that are branded. These include your brand name, taglines, slogans or other branded terms that reflect your brand names and sentiments. Because branded hashtags are specific to your brand, they will tend to have much smaller usage numbers which will grow over time as your brand awareness increases. Have some fun with these hashtags while still focusing on being pertinent to your target audience. There is no need to be overly conservative in this regard since a little fun associated with your brand is always a good thing!

The second bucket of hashtags that you will need to create is your product hashtags. This is where you can include hashtags of specific products or gear such as #wearable or #wearabletech that helps your target customer identify a type of product or product attributes, as well as take advantage of the search volume of some of the more popular hashtags. This is also a great place for hashtags that have a product function focus such as #sportswatch because some customers care a lot more about the utility than anything else. While many of these types of hashtags tend to be quite popular (used millions of times such as #watch used 21 million times), there is often a more targeted and relevant hashtag like the aforementioned examples which tend to be less popular (used hundreds of thousands or thousands of times), so there is a nice balance of both.

The final bucket for hashtags focuses on location. Using hashtags specific to your community or where your business is located is a great way to connect with people in your surrounding area to make a connection. Many customers love supporting their local businesses, so make the most of location hashtags so you stay top of mind with the people in the closest vicinity. This is also a great way to build community with your target audience because your target audience neighborhood is personal as well as YOU-centric. Location hashtags such as #sandiegoliving can also be effective when your brand is on the go, attending certain event conferences, grand openings or fostering partnerships. So make sure you have identified the best location hashtags and begin using them.

Another important thing to remember when using hashtags is that you want a healthy mix of popular and less popular but more targeted and specific hashtags because your post will be more likely to stand out. This is important because using hugely popular hashtags such as #love (1.3B) will likely mean that you are lost in a sea of this hashtag (it also isn't terribly relevant). Instead, use some popular hashtags (used 1 million times or less) that are appropriate to your business such as #loveyoga. Marry the popular hashtags with less popular hashtags (used hundreds of thousands of times) as well as your branded hashtags which are specific to your brand. This approach allows you to increase your potential reach while measuring which hashtags garnered the most engagement.

Remember that you want the hashtag to be relevant to the post, so don't automatically include all twenty to thirty hashtags. Rather, select the hashtags that are representative of each post. For instance, if you are posting about your new cereal, use product or ingredient specific hashtags, as well as audience hashtags.

@Mentions

While hashtags are used for search visibility, Mentions are used for highlighting partnerships, influencers, gurus or other high profile individuals or brands in your Instagram feed. They are also used to make connections with the aforementioned and give them some love. Utilizing Mentions is a great approach for increasing engagement on your page. Mentions work well because the account or profile that has been mentioned in the post receives a notification, so this is an excellent tactic for creating two-way dialogue (engagement) between the brands and individuals. For instance, if one of your clients is working with a well-known fitness influencer, you might mention him in a post about health and fitness. That Mention then opens the door for the influencer to comment back and mention the brand in the reply. For instance, post "Getting ready for some fitness inspiration from @fitnessguru." @fitnessguru will see the post and will likely reply with something like the following: "Thanks @genericbrand, can't wait to share some tips with you."

That or the influencer can share the post on his Instagram page via a #regram. In either scenario, your brand benefits from the association with the influencer (think of it as social networking) and your brand profile gets additional visibility because now your profile is mentioned on the influencer's feed. This is a YOU-centric tactic because the communication is about the influencer or audience that you're trying to engage with versus your brand.

This tactic also works well in the initial phase of building social media influencer partnerships. In the early stage of building your influencer network, the more you can give some visibility to potential influencers the better. This extra attention makes them feel important and sets a great foundation for moving the relationship forward. Once an influencer agrees to try your product, for instance, this is a great time to thank them with a post and a Mention. For instance, "So excited that you have agreed to try our new running shoes @joeabs. Thank you!" This doesn't mean they will write a great post or review of your sample product, but it certainly puts them on a solid path for doing so. Why not give them an initial shout-out for giving your brand a try?

The other element of this is to actually engage with these brands, gurus or influencer's pages. Jump on their pages regularly and comment on their posts. While this requires work, this is really what social media is about – creating conversations with your target audience or influencers. Plus, Liking and Commenting on their posts helps your brand stay top of mind. This is an excellent way to get them to see your brand as an advocate of their brand, which will make them more likely to follow your brand. Use your YOU-centric effort to open doors to a more significant and meaningful relationship with them.

The truth is, some people will follow your brand just because of your association with influencers, celebrities or other influential brands. While seeking quality over quantity should always be your aim, it isn't bad to have someone to follow you initially based off of this, and then earn their continued follow once they see the value associated with your brand.

Location Tags

Location tags are ideal for highlighting certain businesses that are in alignment with your brand or specific geographies. More importantly, location specific hashtag searches are a common practice on Instagram, so maximize your reach by using location tags. Plus, adding a location tag to your image allows your target audience to see where you took the image, and posts the location on top of the picture. This works particularly well for brick and mortar stores with physical locations because followers are able to find your business. Location tagging is a nice way to keep your brand focused on your local community and vicinity.

Micro-influencers

Another success factor for Instagram is working with relevant social media influencers. Again, finding the right social media influencer takes some effort. First, you have to look at their page to see if their philosophy, content and imagery is in alignment with your brand. Then you have to carefully examine their existing partnerships. For instance, if you sell luggage, you want to be mindful of the influencer's other partnerships with other bag companies. You don't want to create a partnership that has some competitive aspects or is in some way in conflict with your brand. Typically, the influencer would shy away from working with you because of the conflict anyway, but do the homework in advance to avoid wasting your time.

Some people think of influencer relationships as merely just a pay-to-say ploy. They think of it as hiring an influencer and telling the influencer what to post and when. The compensation and the structure is totally dictated by the brand. This is a fine approach but certainly won't cultivate the YOU-centric marketing approach that really drives results. Why? Because influencers are people too. They want to structure partnerships that further their brand and your brand. They want it to be a great fit for them and you. That means they should drive what they post and when. If not, it feels inauthentic to them and their brand, which puts their reputation, engagement, follower count, etc. in jeopardy but also makes it so you will likely never get their best. The truth is, you should treat your influencers with the same care that you treat your other important associations. You should structure your partnerships such that it feels natural and organic to what they already do in terms of their style, approach and posting cadence. That doesn't mean you have an entirely hands-off approach to the brand needs, but start by having them outline what they would like to do with your brand. You can then work with them on any special extras or creative elements that you think are important, but realize that if they have a strong following, they have it for a reason, so when in doubt, trust their judgment. This sets the stage for a lasting partnership.

There is certainly a lot of buzz about what influencers can do for your brand in terms of reach and engagement, but the important thing to consider is at what cost? Getting a famous celebrity to mention you on social media would be tremendously impactful, but at what expense and how often could he/she do it before your budget is exhausted?

In working with our clients, we always focus much of our efforts on micro-influencers. Micro-influencers are up and coming influencers who have smaller follower counts but still have tremendous sway with their followers. Micro-influencers tend to serve a more targeted or niche audience with more engaged communities but have follower counts in the tens of thousands versus the hundreds of thousands or millions. The beauty of micro-influencers is that they have an authenticity and genuineness often not found in those who have already reached celebrity status. They also care about their follower's needs and wants so they are the ideal YOU-centric relationship.

They may also offer a highly targeted audience that they love to share new, relevant products with. Micro-influencers, like other social media influencers, want to partner with brands that support their ideals, values and interests. They want to offer their audience true value. They don't want to risk their hard-earned online reputation. Can you blame them? That means fostering a partnership with them must provide a real benefit to their audience as well as elevate their brand. They won't partner with just anyone, so it is important that you treat them as the valuable partners that they are.

The other benefit of working with micro-influencers is that their rates are far more reasonable. Many micro-influencers are willing to post on your behalf for hundreds of dollars versus thousands. This means that even small businesses can partner with micro-influencers. The only trick is finding the right influencers to partner with. We recommend performing searches based on relevant keywords or terms for your brand and see what influencers pop up.

Imagery

The final element for success on Instagram (this is an ever-evolving platform so this list will never be entirely complete) is to let your imagery tell a story. If you are posting a product shot or lifestyle shot, tell the story behind the shoot. Who was involved and what happened? Behind the scenes commentary about your image is a great way to further engagement because most brands only share the perfect image and not how they got it. This approach also applies to your lifestyle image. Share why the image is important or what it means to you. Where was it shot and why did you pick the location? While this may sound like it differs from a YOU-centric approach, it is actually because your brand is sharing information that your audience can connect with through storytelling.

Think of it like this: I'm flipping through my social media feed and see product image after product image, none wildly different from the next, when suddenly I see one that reads: "We took this picture after a long, hot day in the desert sun to remind us that a little effort always leads to an even bigger reward" and it is a picture of your product with an amazing sunset behind it. How different do you feel seeing and reading that versus, "Our product is packed full of #vitamin D."

With that said, your Instagram images should be much more than product shots. If not, it feels too much like a sales pitch. You want to use your product or promotional shots sparingly (around 20% of the time). Don't be like so many brands that think their customers want to be exposed to their products 24/7. They don't. They want to be exposed to the things that matter to them.

Of course, it isn't just the caption that matters. The imagery is really at the top of the priority list because on Instagram it must be beautiful. But Instagram has an ocean of stunning imagery. That means you need to do more than just post captivating images, you need to tell your story through the pictures on the page. Don't worry, it's fun once you get the hang of it!

Instagram Checklist to Increase Engagement

@mention	Include gurus, influencers and partnerships in posts
Location tag	Include location tags in posts
@user tag	Tag people in photos
Call To Action (even if just asking a question)	Included in every post
Commenting/Replying to posts	Comment on other people or brands' posts and always respond to post comments within 24 hours.
Branded hashtags	Add your list of branded hashtags
Relevant hashtags (based on post content)	Use relevant hashtags
Brand mentions (when possible, such as REI)	Include complementary brands
Instagram Stories/IGTV	Use to show behind-the-scenes aspects of your brand
Photo Orientation (portraits too)	Use portrait and landscape

Chapter 13: **Facebook**

If you have been paying attention to your Facebook business page performance, you know that your organic reach has been taking a hit. In fact, studies have found that organic reach on Facebook now sits in the single digits, and brands with large follower numbers (500K) have felt the biggest impact. While the decline in organic reach has been happening for the last few years, the biggest impact occurred when Facebook changed the algorithm in 2018 to prioritize "meaningful interactions."

So what exactly are meaningful interactions? Facebook's top ranking factors include comments, reactions (love emoji, anyone?), and sharing content via the platform or their Messenger app. This means you can no longer get away with simply securing Likes on your post and calling it a day. Rather, your content has to engage someone enough that they are willing to comment or share, and it makes sense when you think about it. It is far easier to simply click the Like button when scrolling through your feed and then move on, whereas actually stopping to comment or share means that the content elicited a much stronger reaction, which is exactly the kind of feeling Mark Zuckerberg wants to drive.

This change equates to marketers needing to move away from a product-centric or brand-first approach and into a customer or YOU-centric focused approach. No wonder Facebook users report disliking too much promotional content from brands. There is a surfeit of this product-centric content on Facebook these days.

These posts are all about the brand and not about the audience. The truth is that you aren't going to create much conversation if the concentration is on your brand goals alone. As such, your strategy needs to shift and concentrate on your customers. Think posts that educate your target audience or provide informative value, posts that inspire, or posts that entertain. In fact, according to a recent study from Sprout Social, 59% of consumers want the post to teach them something. Remember, What is in it for me? In addition to that interesting stat, 30% want a link to more information. Now think about that! Who doesn't want to look smart to their friends?

To build an effective strategy, you need to dig into the analytics of your page and really understand your followers' interests. While you should start with the demographics of your audience, it is important that you take it one step further and understand the brands that your Facebook fans like, the gurus they follow, and the websites they frequent. We recommend directing your attention to the niche or more targeted, lesser known elements that your followers like. Knowing that they love a lesser known personality like Nick Ortner, for instance, is more valuable than knowing that they love Oprah in terms of really understanding where their specific interests lie. Once you understand the analytics of the page, move onto the content strategy. Ask what types of content will provide the most insight and engagement for this audience. Be all about them, and create something that feels personalized to your target audience. This can prove tricky because people seek out and consume different content, but there are some good rules to follow.

Video

We have said it before and we will say it again – video is naturally engaging and should be included in your Facebook strategy. Facebook Live is all the rage right now, and this is an ideal approach if you can pull it off. If not, create other types of videos that connect with and provide helpful information to your audience. People love to share content like behind-the-scenes videos of your business (the real, raw stuff), or you could tell a compelling version of your customers' story, or create a compelling how-to video. Remember, even a video shot on your mobile phone can be extremely engaging (remember the Chewbacca mask Mom?). It doesn't have to be professionally produced. When done right, video is the ideal YOU-centric storyteller. It takes a little upfront planning, but it is well worth the time and energy.

Curating Content

Reposting or sharing others' valuable content is another wise strategy. Seek out your industry leaders or influencers and share their richest content with your audience. Create a consistent schedule around curating and sharing this content such that your followers come to expect to receive it. This is an excellent way to associate your brand with the authority and influence of someone else while providing high quality content. Think of it as social networking. While this won't drive traffic to your site, it will improve your engagement by sharing curated content that matters to your audience.

Facebook Groups

Joining or starting your own Facebook Group is another great way to foster engagement. Utilizing Groups allows you to be part of the conversation within your industry or target market. Even better, Groups can be centered around a specific topic, lifestyle, product/service or brand so there are many opportunities to test out which Group works the best for your company. We love seeing brands start their own Group because this is an excellent environment to nurture and engage your customers with helpful advice, offer Q&As, and build customer loyalty. It is an excellent venue for YOU-centric communication. After all, any strategy worth its salt is all about creating community. Joining or creating Groups allows your brand to do just that.

Advertising

Of course, we all know there is more than one reason for the changes to organic reach, and certainly increasing Facebook's ad revenue (which has also increased in cost) is one of the main drivers. The truth is that you really can't avoid advertising on Facebook if you're in need of brand awareness (and many brands are in need of this). Facebook is an amazing advertising platform when you really know and understand your target audience. Even though the cost to advertise is steadily increasing, it still offers an affordable approach to reaching your target audience.

The one thing that is important to remember with Facebook is that it is used best to introduce and reinforce your brand. We rarely recommend utilizing Facebook to drive conversions exclusively. That doesn't mean it can't happen, but it means it's a slow slug on Facebook. First, you have to spend a good amount of time and money creating brand awareness and interest then eventually that brand awareness will result in sales. It does happen eventually, but you can use other channels more quickly and effectively to close business than you can on Facebook.

However, virtually every brand could use a little challenge in terms of upping their game and really driving engagement through Facebook. No one said it would be easy, but with some strategic thought, YOU-centric focus, and creativity, these efforts will separate your brand from the competition and create raving fans.

Instagram Checklist to Increase Engagement

@mention	Include gurus, influencers and partnerships in posts
Call to action (a little encouragement goes a long way)	Ask fans to share and comment on your posts
Commenting/Replying to posts	Always respond to post within 24 hours.
Video	Use video as often as possible
Branded hashtags	Add your list of branded hashtags
Posting frequency	Increase posting frequency
Ask Friends to Like the Page	Invite your friends and family to participate

Chapter 14: **Search Marketing**

Even search is not immune to the personalized needs of today's customer. In fact, one of the biggest areas of focus for brand marketers utilizing successful search strategies is to understand the intent of your target audience. Yes, even search queries have become more personalized, more YOU-centric. People use search engines to get information and advice that is specific to their individual needs and wants. They realize that being specific in their search delivers more relevant results. They're also increasingly using terms like "I" and "me" in their search terms because again, they are looking for relevance to themselves.

In addition, search queries have become more localized or customized because today's consumers crave convenience and ease in purchasing. It is for this reason that search terms with the words "shopping near me" or "when to buy" and other intention searches are increasing year-over-year on Google. Keep this in mind when developing your keyword strategy. Just like other YOU-centric tactics, the more you know about the needs, desires and interests of your customers, the more successful you will be in targeting the right audience through organic and paid search.

Let's be clear, if you are an ecommerce brand who relies on traffic to your website, search marketing is going to have to be part of your strategy because you have to have strong visibility on search engines. You also have to drive qualified traffic to your website. With that said, you need to approach search with your eyes wide open. For starters, paid search engine marketing, or pay-per-click, is not child's play. You need a seasoned expert to set up, adjust and monitor your campaigns. This isn't something that anyone can do or that can be self-taught without a lot of lost money, opportunity, time and heartache. So do yourself a favor and hire someone with a track record of success.

In addition, depending on the competitiveness of the industry, realize that PPC (Pay-Per-Click) can be a break-even proposition, and more specifically, and within some fields and companies break-even is the new measurement for success. PPC can also be outside the budget for small businesses or start-ups that have to compete against large, big budget brands. Of course, most industries are still seeing a strong ROI (return on investment) from search engine marketing, but it largely depends on your margins if paid search is the right choice for your brand. With that said, Google reports that for every $1.00 spent brands are still making a $2.00 on average. For this reason, you need to have realistic expectations, but also understand that paid search continues to be the best marketing option for driving conversions. Plus, the game with paid search is that once you capture a customer, it is a lot easier to keep them as a customer (assuming that you treat them well) and that is where PPC really delivers the return. The lifetime value of the customer far exceeds the acquisition cost.

Another important lever of search is Organic search or Search Engine Optimization (SEO). While organic search has experienced a lot of changes over the years and this is a segment that is ripe with myths, SEO should be included in your brand's YOU-centric marketing mix. Once again, you have to have an expert in this regard, and unfortunately, many organic search firms claim to be experts but are far from it. Watch out for anyone claiming they will guarantee first page search engine results (in fact, if you hear this, run for the hills). Anyone can get you on the first page for some obscure term with miniscule traffic, and the ability to pull that off doesn't make them an SEO expert.

What is important to remember is that SEO is all about the content and keywords. Specifically, you are looking for keywords and phrases that have a decent monthly search volume (1,000 to 10,000), low competition, and organic click-through rates, which is an estimated number of organic clicks in search engine results. This combination of data points delivers the sweet spot in terms of which keywords you should utilize within your YOU-centric content strategy.

These keywords should be used in your blogs or content assets as well as throughout your website. This doesn't mean you should load up your content with keywords (that is a serious search engine no-no) but rather use a few keywords that fit naturally into the content and are relevant to your target audience. For instance, seek out keywords that describe your product's attributes, such as "multivitamins for women" as well as phrases that include commercial intent or purchase intent such as "buy" or "best." The latter tends to signal that the customer is closer to the bottom of the funnel, or ready to buy. Your strategy will also want to factor the impact of "featured snippets" such as Google's answer boxes which offer consumers the convenience of skipping the click to your website's URL and instead providing an immediate answer. This is where the aforementioned quizzes or other interactive content can be your best friend because the user needs to click or engage with the content to receive the sought after answers.

The most important thing to consider when diving into SEO is that like everything else in digital marketing, it is always changing based on the latest algorithm changes. In fact, the biggest change to come will occur with voice search. While it is too early to know the exact impact of voice search, rest assured your SEO strategy will need to change as a result. That means your SEO expert also needs to be well-versed on the latest trends and industry occurrences. However, this is an easy criteria to vet. Simply ask them what they read and study on a regular basis. You can also ask about the latest algorithms to impact SEO, and if they don't have an answer, move on.

Search is important because you need to have a presence online, and you need to drive traffic – qualified traffic that is – to your website. Search is essential for sending qualified traffic to your site. However, it doesn't stop there. The next step is to drive customer conversions through a YOU-centric approach because traffic for traffic's sake won't get you very far, while understanding how to attract and retain customers will.

SEO Checklist:

This type of information is accessible through SEO keyword tools or from your SEO specialist.

Keywords
Best multivitamin for women over 50

Monthly Search Volume
1,900

Keyword Difficulty
57.61
(the lower the number the better).

CPC
$1.21
The average U.S. advertising price companies pay for a users click for an ad triggered by these keywords.

SERP Features
1
(this is an important number because it reflects the number of features – Google's self-hosted solutions which includes "featured snippets" and answer boxes for the given keywords on the search results page which can keep users on Google versus clicking on a given URL in search results)

Chapter 15: **Maximizing Influencer Marketing**

The Influencer Marketing industry is predicted to reach as high as $10 billion dollars in 2020. In other words, if your brand isn't using influencer marketing currently then you should be. Influencer marketing is when your brand hires a social media guru or individual with a significant following on social media to promote your brand. Influencer marketing works because real, normal people have built a following online that trusts what they say. That gives them considerable sway. Influencers understand the importance of this, and they work diligently to keep their followers happy and engaged. This makes influencer marketing inherently YOU-centric because most successful influencers care deeply about what their audience likes and appreciates. Brands that understand this can benefit greatly by partnering with influencers. So the question is not whether to work with influencers, but rather, how soon can you start?

Influencer marketing is an ideal YOU-centric marketing opportunity for most brands large or small because of the range of influencers (macro to micro in scope), but structuring (and fulfilling) an effective influencer marketing strategy takes work; there is much to think through. In the chapter on Instagram, micro-influencers were covered in some detail, but there is more to the story than just setting up the right partnership. There is also the start of the discussion, the why behind your influencer marketing strategy. Finding the right influencer is the easy part.

Your brand needs to begin by thinking through and determining the goals of your influencer marketing strategy. Are you seeking to further your brand awareness and reach a new or broader audience? Are you looking to drive traffic and leads? Is your most important metric engagement? You need to determine your goals for adding influencer marketing to your marketing mix.

There needs to be clearly defined objectives and something to measure against. If you don't have one or two goals that justify what you are using influencer marketing to achieve, you will quickly find yourself with an ocean of influencers that are going in every direction except the one you want. Don't under-estimate this channel. Remember, it is only getting larger and more nuanced. In fact, influencer marketing can become unruly if you don't start with a specific set of outcomes/goals and use that as the baseline for determining where to focus your efforts.

Start with a plan, and an ability to track that plan. Your brand needs to define how you will measure success. Will website traffic and social mentions be measurements? Will link building? How about opt-ins or sales? The analytics will be an important driver that you will need to track and monitor. Now is also a good time to look into data solutions. Companies such as SproutSocial and Later offer social analytic tools as do many influencer platforms/ networks such as AspireIQ. Our firm recommends a combination of social tools and dashboards, as none seem to provide the depths of information that we seek. Nonetheless, your brand will need to regularly review, analyze and utilize the data to be effective at influencer marketing so do yourself a favor and invest in one or more social analytic tools.

The next step is thinking through the different ways you can use influencers to enhance your brand. This can be viewed from the lens of an individual campaign or an overarching strategy with a series of campaigns. There will be some degree of consistent tactics that you will likely execute regularly, but this will give you a chance to see the 360 degree view. There are three different ways to structure your influencer relationships or campaigns. First, there is the product exchange or free approach. Typically, these occur with the influencer reaching out to the brand and seeking product in exchange for a post or posts on their social media page. This relationship tends to come from an influencer who may already be a fan of your brand and tends to offer a smaller audience or lower follower count. There are also some influencers who will give you a shout out on their page for free.

The second type of influencer relationship is to pay an influencer to create posts about your brand and products. Most companies tend to use these as one-offs (posting one or two times) where they have many influencers posting once. This is fairly common with brands that just want to reach a lot of different influencer audiences quickly. The price per posts ranges based on follower count and niche.

The third type is a retainer agreement between the brand and the influencers. These are often referred to Brand Ambassadors who also receive free products and a consistent presence with your brand. Relationships of this nature tend to occur with more well-known or larger influencers. Please note: Influencers like these the best and for obvious reasons. For one, retainer relationships are longer in duration. A brand doesn't tend to retain an influencer for a month. They retain an influencer for 6 months or year or beyond. Brands do this when they really want to be associated with the influencer and they understand the value of repetition in marketing. This structure also affords the opportunity for different creative assets to be used such as video, takeovers or guest blogging which allows for greater continuity between the brand and the influencer as well as fresh content creation. The other benefit is that the influencer's audience really gets to know the brand and gains a firmer affinity or appreciation based on the longer-term association. Of course, not all brands can do this, but it is certainly wise to consider if you can.

Once the type of relationship has been defined with the influencer it is now time to think about the strategy to use. Are you seeking sponsored content or something more elaborate like a recipe utilizing your product? Do you want to create an affiliate relationship with your influencers where they receive compensation for opt-ins and sales or does your brand merely provide them with discount codes? Do you want the influencer to attend a certain event? Your brand might only be looking for social mentions or an influencer to promote a giveaway. The point being there are many different strategies to use with influencers along with a steady stream of new ideas. So have fun with it for the love of Pete! The creativity is part of the joy. Our firm has found that influencers love to collaborate. Make sure your brand embraces this.

Finding the Right Partnerships

Now you can focus on determining which influencers will be the best fit for reaching your target customer. This can be as simple as searching relevant hashtags for your business and seeing which influencers are using them. You can also use relevant keywords and look for influencers associated with the terms. Another approach is to do some influencer searches via your favorite search engine. Bloggers are another class of influencers who have built up their followers based on producing engaging content. As such, they're another great choice and worthy of a potential influencer partnership. The same can be said for thought leaders or industry experts. They are influencers too, and should be added to your possible partner list. You can also use services like Alexa or influencer platforms such as Tribe. There are many options in this regard. You will find it fairly straightforward, and don't worry, you will likely have more choices than your brand needs.

The next step is to evaluate the influencer in terms of their voice, beliefs, passions and interests to ensure that they are in alignment with your brand. At Think, we always start by following the influencer to see what they post, their caption style and imagery. This gives us a chance to get to know them a bit prior to reaching out to them. The influencer also appreciates this approach because, if you have been engaging with their posts, you will have already built some rapport with them and have a greater propensity to create a strong partnership. That may seem like an obvious suggestion, but you would be surprised at how many brands instant message influencers (also a no-no) with generic emails such as "love your content" when they have actually never seen it. The influencer isn't fooled, and this tactic starts the conversation on the wrong foot and likely won't materialize into a fruitful partnership. The other miss that brands sometimes make is that they fall in love with an influencer from afar because they have heard of the influencer, but they haven't actually seen or studied their work. For instance, some influencers use scantily clad photos of themselves on the beach or working out as constant fodder for their feed. That may drive a lot of new followers and interest, but it might be an odd fit for your brand especially if bathing suits and skimpy fitness gear have little to do with your brand.

Put in the upfront work to find the right influencers, and it will pay off. The important thing to remember is that influencer marketing works because it is authentic. Followers of Instagram "celebs" (and that is what they are to their followers, mini-celebrities), believe and trust their influencer of choice. They see him/her brand endorsements as an extension of the influencer. The audience loves the influencer, and as such, they love all that he/she represents including your brand. That is pretty powerful stuff to a brand that wants to really connect with their audience. As a result, the more you respect the genuineness of the partnership the better it will perform.

The final point to remember is that finding the right influencers is based on the audience that they are reaching. Don't be moved by follower count alone. A huge follower count of young male millennials will not move the needle for your brand if you are trying to connect with middle aged women. Carefully examine the influencers audience and determine if they are the right audience for your brand. Our firm also recommends a diversified mix of influencers. Look for varying ages, ethnicities and market focus that have application to your products and brands. For instance, targeting just fitness-oriented influencers for a product that is health and exercise focused may be the best place to start, but your brand should add in other healthy lifestyle influencers to expand your reach and brand awareness. This ensures that your brand doesn't fall into the one trick pony category, and it engages new audiences that may not be familiar with your brand. Talk about a win-win.

If you have yet to jump into influencer marketing, below are a few questions to ask prior to forging a partnership with an influencer. These questions will give you and your team the background and understanding needed to structure a successful influencer marketing relationship from the start:

Questions to Ask an Influencer

1. How do you determine which brands you work with?
2. How do you like to work with brands?
3. What resonates with you with regard to our brand?
4. Why do you want to work with us?
5. Are you willing to attend events on our brand's behalf?
6. What is your average engagement rate?
7. What is your audience reach and why do you think your fans follow you?
8. What does your audience tend to respond to the best – videos, recipes, guest blogging, takeovers, etc?
9. What are some of the unique ways that you have worked with brands?
10. How has working with brands evolved for you over the years?
11. What have been some of your most successful or effective influencer marketing campaigns?
12. What other brands are you currently working with?
13. Are you part of an influencer network or platform?
14. What type of analytics do you provide?
15. What do you recommend in terms of the length of our partnership based on driving maximum success?

Chapter 16: **Manual vs Automation –
The Art of Optimization**

A YOU-centric approach doesn't just apply to certain elements of your marketing strategy. It is equally required across multiple marketing platforms as an omnichannel strategy. Your brand has to start with a YOU-centric focus to know what is resonating with your clients and then optimize those aspects that are driving the best results. However, this is where it can get confusing. We often think of optimization as automated intelligence or machine learning, and while that is a form of optimization, it isn't that whole story. In fact, many brands wrongfully assume that once you determine and master the YOU-centric connection-building between your brand and your audience then it is time to take that data or knowledge and hand it over to a machine to do what they do best; optimize the findings and deliver peak performance.

However, peak performance is where this thought-process falls flat. The appeal is understandable, in the fast-paced world of tech, it can be compelling to look for automation to take some of the workload off of your digital marketing efforts, and there are certain tasks that can be effectively automated. However, while this sounds good in theory, in a broader context it often produces lackluster results. There simply is no substitute for human eyes, manual oversight, investigation and on-going optimization. This is particularly true when applying a YOU-centric strategy because the analysis and understanding of the data is crucial to your results.

That means that an optimization expert needs to be reviewing, examining, and scrutinizing the data on a regular basis (and by regular basis, we're talking daily examination) to make sure that your marketing is delivering your brand's performance objectives.

Automation is often praised as the cure-all to all of your brand's digital marketing woes. It is considered the ideal way to scale and meet your brand's performance goals at a lower cost. Moreover, firms or ad agencies that rely on automation often claim to produce similar results. More often than not, automation is portrayed to be just as effective in producing strong online marketing performance as manual or human optimization. Don't be fooled. I can't tell you how many times my firm has been pitched on using, or approached about using, an automated service solution to track social media hashtags of interest and offer programmed commenting on those relevant hashtags. This is sold as an opportunity to seamlessly grow your business's follower count without any of the manual work involved. The idea being that the robot will follow certain hashtags and comment on your business' behalf on social media. It works by asking you to pre-determine which comments you would like the bot to make on behalf of your business. That is why you see so many smiling face or fire emojis or comments that seem irrelevant to your post such as the "nice," "cool," or "love your page". The premise being that once the account(s) that you targeted via a certain hashtag such as #buzzfeast sees your comments on their posts that they will then follow your account because you engaged with their content and hashtag. Oh, if it only worked that way.

First, this type of automated service actually violates the terms of social media platforms. It isn't surprising that platforms such as Instagram and Facebook frown upon fake comments from bots versus real human interaction. The whole point of social media is to create human connections. Second, this approach is beyond obvious to the account that receives the comment. Imagine if your Facebook business page account posted something heartfelt or even sorrowful on a post such as the passing of an industry mentor only to receive a fire emoji in response. It not only doesn't drive the desired outcome, it is off-putting. More than that, one can tell that it isn't authentic so there is little chance that you would follow the account that engages in such low-brow tactics. Nonetheless, services that offer automated commenting on social media abound because of the perception that it works just as well as human interaction. Specifically, these services sell the idea that they can quickly, as well as easily, increase your follower count without the cumbersome expense of actual human oversight. Even if the brand did see some incremental follower lift, they would likely see the increase quickly fade away as the people who followed them because of the commenting would likely unfollow when they discover that the content is not relevant to them. Regardless, some wrongly believe that automation is the answer to all that ails the brand in the realm of digital marketing, including growing your social media presence.

This inaccurate assumption isn't just happening on the social media front. My company had a similar experience with paid search. I was in the process of hiring a paid search expert, and I scheduled an interview with one of the candidates. His background seemed ideal for working at my firm, Think Media. The interview was going quite well when I asked him to describe his optimization approach. He gleefully exclaimed that he didn't need to optimize paid search campaigns. Rather, he let Google's algorithm do the work, and he just focused on the campaign set-up. To say that the interview ended shortly thereafter would be an under-statement. I can't imagine explaining that we hired a paid search specialist that only knows how to set-up a campaign but not how to actively manage or optimize for the best performance. However, to this individual the answer of automation seemed perfectly acceptable.

The allure of using technology to gather and consume the data and then using more technology to automate the optimization process is real. It feels like a no-brainer to some. Why not use tech to manage tech? Machines know everything, right? That means you can just set and forget your digital marketing efforts, and all will be well. Please no. The truth is that the secret to digital marketing success is to regularly optimize the most important aspects of your campaign towards your primary objective. For example, if your goal is to drive conversions via search, then all of your efforts need to be focused on achieving that goal. This would require consistent methodology as well as regular management aimed toward search conversion. If your goal is to increase your ad campaigns impressions then you need to optimize toward that, and so on.

Automation simply has not advanced to a point where it can adequately handle the complexities of optimizing campaigns effectively. Constant review is required. Take just the audience segments as an example. An expert will review the performance over time and remove or replace segments based on the performance. This is just one element to consider. There are optimization opportunities with bid adjustments, budget adjustment, etc. There are innumerable critical elements to your marketing success. A social ad or paid search budget can quickly get eaten up only to deliver poor performance, and if your team is not actively managing it to see if the performance warrants the budget allocation, then you're doing your brand a huge disservice and wasting your precious ad budget.

We haven't even touched on ad frequency or conversion funnels. There is also keyword optimization. There needs to be constant evaluation of your brand's best performing keywords. There needs to be a concentration on eliminating low performing keywords and adding new keywords to the marketing mix. The point being that there are many things to optimize or ways to improve performance.

Of course, there are some benefits to using automation in some cases, especially if you have a limited budget and your team lacks the necessary skill. It is a decent option for companies that are just starting out and they want to dip their toe in the water, so to speak. It can also be an effective way to test lower budget campaigns. There are also advances being made in machine learning and artificial intelligence which could change this equation in the future, and make it more viable for larger advertising spends, but we aren't there yet. Remember, you get what you pay for. We often find ourselves having this discussion when clients ask us about our rates for paid search or social advertising management. The client is often perplexed because our rates may be higher than some "other firms, but the cost is a reflection of a skilled professional optimizing the campaigns versus a machine. It takes time, resources and seasoned expertise to deliver a strong advertising performance. Unfortunately, there is no shortcut or substitute. Expert paid search and social strategists do not tend to come inexpensively.

Effective optimization also doesn't tend to be fast. It typically takes a few months of study, exploration, and analysis before the projected performance, but that is ultimately what makes clients happy – hard work and optimal results. What customer doesn't love that?

The truth is that there is no substitute for a digital marketing specialist performing optimization on behalf of your business. These experts understand the art of optimization. Namely that it takes constant analysis, adjustments, targeting and testing to get your campaigns to produce an impressive return. Do your brand a favor and skip the robot in favor of the human, you'll be much more pleased with the outcome.

Chapter 17: **Data, Data, Data**

In an age that values big data, it is understandable why the issue of privacy is on so many people's minds. Let's face it, big data can be creepy. Corporations know, and can share, not just your favorite cereal with the world but also the name of your dog. Regardless of how you feel about it, big data isn't going anywhere. What is not clear is your brand's responsibility with the data. How should brands use data to serve their purposes while still safeguarding or factoring in your consumer's rights? Those are big questions to ask without easy answers, but the first step is realizing the enormity of what you are dealing with in terms of people's information. Your brand needs to be very transparent about using, as well as capturing, the data. Think privacy policies and cookie notifications.

If you're not entirely sure what big data means, not to fear. Big data is comprised of three things: machine, social and transactional data. Social data is the most straightforward and provides critical insights on sentiments, opinions, causes, and thoughts. Machine data (machine learning is a subset of Artificial Intelligence) is becoming, by the day, more of a game-changer with significant impact on the data that it monitors and tracks. Transactional data connects the dots by revealing what your customers purchase. That means there is little left to keep "private." With that said, data, like everything else, can be used or misused.

The fact is that your brand sits on a wealth of data whether you purchase supplemental information or just use your own business data. Even smaller or newly established brands can use their website analytics, social media data, and email list to determine their audience as well as their interests. Larger established brands will have access to additional data that goes beyond websites, email lists, social media and into things such as customer surveys, focus groups, sales, heatmaps and every other data point. All of which can be used to really take a deep dive into your customer, and deep dive is exactly what your brand should do.

However, as noted previously, YOU-centric marketing isn't just about knowing your audience, it is also about understanding your audience. Knowing and understanding are two very different things. As such, it is important to look at each of the data points separately to really see the differences in the data or the things that surprise you. The rule of thumb in our firm is to always seek to answer the question, "so what?" Specifically, what does the data tells us? What does it mean? What are the tangible steps that we can take to improve our business based on what the data conveys? This is when data is really powerful, when it can be applied directly to improving your business.

The first step to understanding your data is to truly understand your demographics. I know this sounds basic, but it is important to note the differences in demographics within your social data and your website. More often than not, they aren't exact replicas of one another. That may mean that you aren't converting your social media audience or it may mean that your social media marketing efforts aren't reaching or engaging the right audience. Either way, swift action needs to be taken, and you can't take that action if you don't look at the data in isolation at the beginning stage of the process.

Knowing the demographic data is a must, but reviewing that data alone will not be that helpful in understanding how to truly connect with your target audience in a YOU-centric way. The reason being that people are far more unique than their age, income level, gender, education, and occupation would suggest. To truly understand your customer's values, interests, opinions, attitudes and behaviors, otherwise known as your customer's psychographics, requires a more thorough examination and thoughtful methodology. This type of data is more subjective than the aforementioned demographic data. Thus, it requires more resources, times and cost to examine and understand this data, and often that is why brands avoid going deeper into their customer analysis. Hiring a firm to do a focus group, for instance, can be expensive.

Fortunately, there are other options which provide great insight. Tools such as customer surveys via platforms like Survey Monkey or interviewing your ideal target customer to learn more about their specific values (which was covered in previous chapters) are great options. However, there must be great care given to the framing of the questions to ensure that your questionnaire isn't driving a pre-determined, desired response. The answers need to be an accurate reflection of your customer's truthful sentiments.

Social media is an outstanding tool for understanding your customer's psychographic data in detail. A review of Facebook's ad targeting options helps to paint an astonishing picture of the power of accessing this information. An examination of just the Interest Targeting on Facebook reflects a wealth of information; everything from family and relationships, to hobbies/activities, shopping and fashion, entertainment and more. Knowing what interests your customer in terms of hobbies, family and shopping tells you a great deal about him or her even outside of layering in other data. That means your brand can really hone in on who your customer is and what matters to them.

Your brand can also use Facebook to explore your customer's purchase behavior, politics, device usage, interest in upcoming events, etc. Think about how much more you can learn about your customer when you explore this type of data. It will educate you on what your customers care about. Now layer that data with the interest data, demographics, as well as location data, and your brand is really starting to cook with gas. The point is that Facebook has an enormous amount of personal information about your target audience which your brand can use to better understand your customer. Twitter is also an amazing resource for identifying and understanding your audience's personal interest. There are also social listening or monitoring tools such as Mention, which makes it easy to see what your customers and others are saying about your brand, including the sentiment trends of your brand. That is yet another data asset in your market research tool belt. The only thing to remember is that the goal is to provide an interesting, YOU-centric or personal experience that resonates and feels welcomed to your target customer, because it is relevant to them. It isn't about intrusion or an invasion of privacy but rather germaneness.

Reviewing your brand's Google analytics is another strong tool for understanding the interests of your audience. You can learn a great deal by looking at the content on your website that is receiving the most interest but also by appraising the audience flow and noting where the visitors are dropping off or exit your website. Both show what is of interest and what is not, or whether there is a cumbersome element to your website navigation. Another valuable Google tool is the Affinity Categories within Google Analytics which conveys visitor interests. Comparing and contrasting this information with Google Trends is another resource able to dissect what topics are of interest as it relates to searches that are trending within your industry and customer interests. You can use this to supplement your content with current developments, but it is also a great way to tie your content into relevant happenings (a must for brands that wish to look and remain cutting edge. It also gives your team insight on the perceptions, news and occurrences that can impact your brand. Alexa also offers compelling data points to evaluate when wanting to know more about your target audience. And then there is your email list data. There is more data to be investigated there too.

The market research that is highlighted here is just a sampling of the data that is largely available at your fingertips. It doesn't go into the data that can be gleamed from data services such as Nielsen and other powerhouse firms that offer proprietary research (at a significant cost) as well as platforms such as Tableau which helps you understand your data in a succinct dashboard. BuzzSumo is another tool that shows you what types of content, within your business niche, across the web is resonating with your audience or being shared across social media. As such, there are ample data sources or market research to examine and apply to your brand. However, do not fall down the trap that so many brands descend into, namely having vast amounts of data that never gets reviewed, examined or implemented. There is such a thing as data paralysis or too much of a good thing. Your brand can avoid this by looking for commonalities in the data as well as by prioritizing the data and determining which is the most important and actionable to your brand.

All of this data combined tells you not only who your customer is, but why they act the way that they do. The beauty of that understanding is that you can utilize what you know about your customer to make them feel important, special and valued. Use the data to connect with your customer by showcasing what is important to them. Make it You-centric. Most brands don't do this because they don't think of it from the customer's perspective. If you put the customer's wants first and use the data to uncover those wants, then you will be one of the elite brands who maximizes their market research.

This is an enjoyable exercise if you approach it as such. After all, what is more exciting then really knowing what your customer needs and desires? Nonetheless, this is an on-going process and can't be left to a once a year, or less, audit of the data. If so, you may find that you're learning the most insightful aspects of your data efforts too late in the process.

Chapter 18: **Customer Acquisition**

Companies like Netflix know the value of a personalized experience online, which is why they share shows that you might like based on your previous viewings. They understand the more relevant the experience to you, the customer, the more likely you will be to engage and purchase. YOU-centric customer acquisition anticipates your customer's needs and the aforementioned companies understand this.

YOU-centric customer acquisition is all about finding the right channels to communicate with and reach your customers through personalized messaging. This requires some trial and error, especially if you are a start-up business and don't have the benefit of historical data or if your past customer acquisition formula loses its effectiveness. Many customer acquisition tactics were outlined in the previous chapter because customer acquisitions start with gaining strong brand awareness and sending qualified traffic and eyeballs to your website via search and social media. The next step is to view what content on your site is getting the most engagement (clicks, page views, referral traffic, and conversions, just to name a few). It requires a deep dive of the analytics to confirm that you're reaching your target audience, and an understanding of what content, products or services resonate with them.

Fortunately, it has never been easier to determine what interests your customers. Everything from your websites analytics and user flow, to email open rates, to social media engagement, to past purchase history is available to your brand. All of these data points should be viewed collectively as to what messaging is connecting with your customers. Once you understand this, you can expand what is working and eliminate what isn't.

Once you understand the data, the next step to customer acquisition is the evaluation phase on the customer journey. This is where you want to have specific content assets that give your customer greater insight as to why your product or service is relevant to them. You can do this by offering ungated content or gated content. Gated content is high-value content that people can't access without sharing the email address or opting-in, which is used as a lead generator. Ungated content is content that provides additional insight which pushes people farther down your customer journey funnel – from top of funnel to middle of funnel without seeking a visitor's email address or requiring an opt-in. Think of ungated content as a gift to your customers in making their purchasing decision easier, and don't worry that it doesn't offer lead generation. While the previously mentioned is not a lead, it gets the visitor one step closer to becoming a buyer, so it is worth the investment. Comparison sheets (comparing your product attributes to another product) are a great example of this. Gated content provides a lead. Once you get the qualified leads, you then turn on your powerful email marketing campaign designed to give subscribers (or people who opted-in) something of greater value. This can be something like exclusive offers or premium content (just for VIPs) that can't be accessed elsewhere, to keep people from unsubscribing and to create raving fans for your brand. In short, customer acquisition happens in steps.

The other important aspect of customer acquisition, and we touched on the concept earlier, is that of quality over quantity. It is equally germane to your digital marketing strategy. Often we hear of clients that are trying to do it all. They're doing pay-per-click, Google Merchant, Google Display, content syndication, social media advertising, affiliate marketing, influencer marketing, plus all the other offline marketing initiatives. They do all of this and wonder why they are struggling with producing results. The reason is that it is very difficult, even with a large, seasoned team, to do all of these things well. As a result, brands that fall into this trap tend to produce mediocre outcomes across the board, yet think of the tremendous time and effort they're expending! They're wearing themselves out, and likely making a sizable investment, only to walk away with meager outcomes. Don't do this. Effective marketing isn't about trying to do all things, it' about strategically selecting the right techniques and doing them exceptionally well.

As such, concentrate on the key tactics for your brand that support one another, and maximize these initiatives by delving deep within them. Structure them such that an individual expert manages and oversees each. Challenge the individual to become a master of one digital marketing specialty exclusively. Don't do what so many brands do by having one person manage multiple platforms. That doesn't work because they are never able to allocate the time to study the data, apply the learnings, make tweaks, and ascend to a virtuoso of their craft. Build a team of true experts, then make sure your team is speaking to one another to maximize your cross-promotional platform synergies.

When we speak within the context of YOU-centric and what is working now, we must do so in terms of what is actually generating customers. At the end of the day, no one really cares about social media Likes, an increase in traffic, or even a new unqualified lead if they aren't driving conversions. This means your marketing efforts will be judged solely on the amount of sales generated and revenue realized. As such, your marketing strategy must focus on customer acquisition. Once you secure the customer, the real work begins with customer retention efforts, but initially, getting and retaining the customer is the top priority. Customer retention is best achieved through making your customers feel honored and appreciated. Frequent and exceptional care is what really makes customers stick with your brand.

Another important factor of customer acquisition is where your business stands in its life cycle. If you are in the start-up phase, you often have to start with things that aren't scalable, such as free samples, demos or trials. This gives your business a chance to acquire new customers to your business but it isn't likely something that you can do in mass or forever, which is fine. You should be seeking areas that work for converting customers, and these strategies will naturally change as the business matures and evolves.

Moreover, there are other things you can do outside of search and social media to boost qualified traffic to your site with the goal of customer acquisition. Let's examine a few more opportunities further.

Affiliate Marketing

It is now time to look at other customer acquisition tactics to expand your brand's reach and visibility. One of the most intriguing and fruitful customer acquisition tactics is affiliate marketing. Affiliate marketing pays a commission to influencers, bloggers or complementary brands to generate sales on your website. The nuts and bolts of affiliate marketing is that you offer a commission (rates can range from 5-30% or even more depending on the product you are selling and your margins) for other brands and influencers promoting your products and sending qualified traffic to your site. The commission is paid out based on your business objectives such as a click, a sign-up or a conversion.

The reason affiliate marketing works is because the other party (blogger, influencer or brand) is incentivized to share your products with their audience. And it works particularly well when the influencer or brand has followers that trust their recommendations. It is for this reason that you don't want to partner with just anyone out there on the affiliate front. You need to work with someone who is truly an advocate of your brand such that their followers will trust the recommendation. It needs to be YOU-centric for the blogger or influencer such that the partnership with your brand is in alignment with who they are. This means you want to be selective and pick affiliate partners that care about your target audience and your brand. This is how your brand will create a true win-win.

Start by identifying affiliates in your space, research their target audience, and make sure that it's a good match. You don't want a bunch of affiliates that aren't representative and champions of your brand because it won't yield positive results. Moreover, we have already discussed how inauthenticity can be felt, so don't even bother going down this path unless you want your affiliate efforts to fail.

Once you have done your homework and selected some strong affiliate partners, don't forget to give them all the resources and love they need to be successful. Remember, this is a YOU-centric relationship. The idea that it takes a village doesn't just apply to raising children, it also applies to growing a successful business.

Referral Marketing and Loyalty Programs

Referral marketing is a great, low-cost customer acquisition tool. Referral marketing allows you to use current happy customers to convert new customers via friends and family. Think of referral marketing as the new loyalty program, albeit loyalty programs and referral marketing are not the same things. Loyalty programs reward customers for their repeat purchases as a way of enticing loyalty and giving more to their high frequency purchasers. This isn't a bad approach, especially because your best customers deserve a little love.

Loyalty programs are often structured as a percentage of the dollars spent to encourage repeat purchases. This works well in a highly competitive market such as gas stations that also tend to operate on low margins. These environments have high frequency purchased products so offering small rewards on each purchase can make your customer feel better about driving an extra few blocks to your gas pump.

While loyalty programs remain effective, they have evolved into something bigger and largely more compelling. Enter Referral marketing. While referral marketing uses some of the same principles as loyalty programs by rewarding their customers, they have a different end game and they appeal to a different type of consumer. Referral marketing works best for brands that already have a strong brand and customer affinity. They also aren't limited to customers with high purchase frequency but still incentivize repeat purchases.

What referral marketing does that is pure genius, however, is that it encourages brand loyalists, or advocates, to refer friends to your business. That makes this tactic YOU-centric because your customers feel good about sharing their favorite brands with the people closest to them. Besides, who doesn't want to share with their friends a brand they adore? This is particularly true of brands that have some level of acclaim associated with them. The other beauty of referral marketing is that they have a high trust factor because your friends wouldn't lead you astray, right? Think of it as automating word-of-mouth referrals, which is something that happens all the time on social media or even in casual conversation, but with a reward for doing what you already do. It is brilliant! Even better, there are some strong players in the market that offer affordable and user-friendly options.

Referral marketing generally offers cash off of your purchase based on engaging in the actions that are most impactful to your business, such as referring a friend, submitting a product review, signing up for enewsletters, and making repeat purchases. This means it works best for brands with higher margins that can afford to shave a bit off of the profits. They can also be used to grow your followers on social media or drive traffic to your website. There really is no shortage of benefits.

Unlike loyalty programs, referral marketing's highest objective is not to retain customers, it seeks to bring new customers to their business without the advertising or marketing cost. Why run expensive advertisements when you could get your happiest customers to refer their friends to your business? Moreover, referral marketing is YOU-centric by its nature because it feels personal and, like your customer, is an integral part of your brand. The best part is that referral marketing works. It drives conversions and can have a significant impact on your business's bottom-line.

The final point in customer acquisition is to narrow your focus on a few tactics that you can execute flawlessly. The approach of doing a little bit of everything because you feel that you must, not only leads to burnout, it also leads to lackluster results. The truth is, you can't possibly do all of these things well. Instead, focus on two to three important tactics and give them your best. If you find that one of the three or all of the three aren't producing the results you seek, change course to focus on the next three tactics as opposed to adding more. You need to concentrate your efforts because acquiring customers takes focus. You don't have time for distractions or throwing a bunch of things at the wall and seeing what sticks. Also, the more focused you are on a few tactics, the more you can dig deep into these tactics, understand the metrics, and really see if your efforts are moving the needle. In our experience, there is always one surefire winner when it comes to customer acquisition, so double down on that effort and master it. There is always time to master another channel or opportunity later.

Chapter 19: **Show Me the Money**

While brands hate to hear this, the truth is that there is no avoiding spending money when it comes to growing your brand and revenues. I get it – everyone loves the story of the company that spent no money and somehow managed to be extremely successful, but the truth is that in today's environment, thinking this is about as close to fantasy as one can get. Sorry, but the old adage that it takes money to make money is true in this regard.

You have to invest in your brand if you want it to succeed, and that investment can come in many forms. You can invest by offering a discount on your product to gain trials. That impacts your margin, but this can be a good strategy, especially if you are new in the market. This doesn't mean you have to discount forever, but it means you are providing some additional incentive to get people to try your product. This is a YOU-centric tactic because more and more customers want to try before committing to a larger purchase. One thing with discounting is that you can't really put the genie back in the bottle after you open it. There will be an expectation set that your brand is willing to discount, but you can use discounting strategically for new product launches, holiday promotions, etc. It doesn't have to be far reaching or a regular occurrence, and we would never suggest otherwise.

The other way to drive conversions is to offer free samples. Again, there is a cost to this investment; namely inventory expense. The truth is, if you believe your product is outstanding, this is a great tactic for driving growth because others are likely to feel the same. This approach also values the customer by saying we believe in our product so much that we are going to take out the risk to you and give the product or service to you. What is even better is that many people are willing to try something for free because of the low barrier to entry, and if you impress them, they will pay for your product. Of course, this is a short-term play, and likely only a small portion of your inventory can be devoted to this initiative (or you may find yourself upside-down). This also creates a sense of urgency with your target audience because it is a limited time and limited inventory offer. Many huge brands have used this approach to great success so consider adding this to your marketing bag of tricks.

If you don't want to discount or give away freebies, you best sit down for this next sentence. You will have to allocate money to both building your brand awareness and increasing conversions. There is no way to sugarcoat this. This is fact. Now, perhaps more than ever, it takes time to build your brand awareness, and that takes money because people want to know, like and trust you before they purchase from you. They also want to make sure your brand meets their individual needs. Think branding. This means not only is producing great, engaging content that speaks to your target audience paramount but so is the repetition. Repetition comes from having a consistent presence on social media, from regularly engaging and growing your email list to connecting with people who are closer to the bottom of the buyer's journey through search via organic and paid efforts. All of this takes money.

The good news is that once you accept this truth, you can go about securing the needed funds to build and sustain your brand. But you should go into this with full understanding and transparency since it takes more money and savvy than you think. Just take Apple, as an example. They refuse to discount or give away their products. It just isn't in their DNA. However, they allocate giant amounts of money to marketing, and with good reason. They also understand the needs, desires and wants of their customers (their messaging is definitely YOU-centric). They know the value of branding and marketing, and they know these efforts bring them customers. Their job is then to just keep producing great products that make their customers' lives easier, and stay the course in terms of their marketing initiatives.

Think about it. That approach is a much better place to be than wrongly assuming that a little marketing will go a long way, then suffering when your product sales are stagnant or non-existent. Get the funds that you need to be successful. Once you do, you can move into the tactical execution of an effective YOU-centric marketing plan.

Chapter 20: **Integrity**

YOU-centric marketing must be authentic and genuine. It must be integrous (honest), and though it isn't often that you see a chapter devoted to integrity in a marketing book, I think it is crucial to your success. In my twenty year career, I have encountered countless times when marketers try to trick, deceive, or otherwise fool their target audience into purchasing their product or participating in their offer. While these instances have often been relatively innocuous, such as a slight misrepresentation, they still lack integrity.

As marketers, our reputations are of the highest importance. So the idea that we would quickly abandon our principles under the guise of doing whatever it takes to make a sale or grow a subscriber list is disappointing. More than that, consumers have been exposed to enough of these shenanigans that they aren't easily fooled. What is worse is when they find out the offer wasn't nearly as spectacular as was promoted, you lose the potential to turn them into a customer, or at least a long-term one.

How many of us have found ourselves purchasing something only to find that the product is rubbish or nothing like it was depicted? I have experienced this. I have eagerly shared my email address and contact information only to find that the download received is of little to no value. It is as though all the thought went into the promotion and not the product (please don't do this). If you are going to put the energy into the promotion, take it one step farther and put the energy into the download, the offer and the product. This is a sure-fire way to start your new customer relationship on the right foot instead of immediately disappointing them or making them feel like a chump for sharing their email with your company to begin with.

The other important aspect of integrity is that it can be felt. Just as you can tell when your friend is being dishonest or disingenuous, you can tell the same with a brand. You may not feel it as intensely, but you know something is afoot whether you can precisely pinpoint it or not. When a brand positions themselves as being something they are not, you know it at some level. How many of us have been exposed to a company that says one thing but does another? These companies rarely develop true brand loyalists. They are out of integrity, and their marketing has that same pungent air about it.

More than that, YOU-centric marketing demands total honesty with your customers. YOU-centric puts the customer first by creating a relationship that you both can feel proud of. You don't want to lose their hard-earned trust, and you don't want to under-cut the work it took to get them to become a customer in the first place.

The truth is that marketing with integrity is worth it. Integrity causes your customers to believe in you (and what is more price-less than that for a brand?), and that credence is one of the things that will keep their loyalty. Gaining customer loyalty also helps to safeguard your brand from your current and future competitors. That trust will also bring them back to your business when they are ready to make a second or third purchase, so don't sell yourself short by using gimmicks that are designed to give a short term gain but long-term pain.

A YOU-centric approach encourages your brand to showcase your brand integrity in all of your marketing and customer service. It says we care about our customers. It says we value our relation-ship enough with you to be truthful. It also says that if you make a mistake (as all humans do), own it and make it right. Put the human in your brand by honoring your commitment to your customers. Lead from a place of absolute integrity and you will be a leader in your field because your brand will feel distinct and noteworthy.

Chapter 21: **Why Consultancy Firms are the New Ad Agency**

Effective marketing is a complex business. It not only requires knowing what is working now, this instant, as well as tomorrow, but also a willingness to change course when what was working no longer works. This means you need a partner that is willing to leave their ego at the door and embrace a constant path of learning. While that might sound obvious, we still encounter seasoned marketers within ad agency firms that profess to know all there is to know and never seek to gain more knowledge. For some reason, some advertising firms purport that their experience alone is what counts rather than staying on top of emerging trends, evolving technologies and new opportunities.

With that said, the goal of this chapter is not to paint anyone in a negative light, because there are many good marketers and great agencies out there. However, the role that ad agencies often play has become less relevant than in the past. Sure, there are times when a great campaign idea is needed or a new creative is in order, and in those cases a savvy ad agency can be your best friend. However, in today's environment, a larger, more strategic partner is needed.

As the owner of a consultancy firm, my business is often mistaken as an ad agency. We don't love it when this happens because clients often have had a less-than-stellar experience or know of someone else's experience where they were "taken" by a bad ad agency. What can we say? It happens. However, the confusion is there for good reason because it can be difficult to identify the differences.

The biggest difference is in the business model. Ad agencies want to secure the business, grow the account by taking on other services/needs, and hold onto the business for as long as possible. There is nothing wrong with that approach, but we believe nimbleness is a necessity, and the goal should be to teach the existing team what is needed to thrive in the changing digital marketing environment. The point being that ad agencies tend to use their own people versus working with the existing marketing team to execute the needed strategies and tactics for success. This means they're in the unenviable role of constantly looking for new ways to grow their business with your brand. That's also why they ask questions like, *Who is doing your media buying?* or *Who handles your branding?* because they would love nothing more than for you to allocate more of your budget to their services. The business model is geared and designed for the long-term because that keeps a steady stream of income coming to their many employees.

Consultancy firms, on the other hand, look at the relationship in terms of what can be gained in the shortest period of time. This doesn't mean they don't want to have a long-term business relationship with your brand, rather, the hope is that your brand won't need to commit indefinite budget resources to the consultancy firm. The goal of consultants is to focus your attention and resources such that you can achieve your brand objectives in a way that allows you to go it alone at some point in the future. We also don't seek out other services to take over because we work with your internal team. Of course, there are times when we need to bring in our team of people and resources, but this is viewed as an immediate fix to a challenge that will be resolved in the future.

The other notable difference is that consultancy firms focus on achieving your goals and objectives. Consultancy firms aren't hired to pitch the next big idea or campaign. They examine the business holistically and determine what's working and what's not. They then elevate what is working and eliminate what is not. They develop a plan based on your specific needs and offer a customized approach. For instance, if you're having difficulty converting customers, they identify areas of confusion for the customers, seek out new opportunities and/or tactics, and make your brand's uniqueness crystal clear. That means the focus is on improving customer acquisition and retention efforts, all while watching the bottom-line.

Consultancy firms aren't seeking to acquire more business from your brand but rather aim to create more business for you by developing strategies and plans to meet your goals. They stay on top of the latest technological advances and what is working by platform to create an integrated approach, which includes everything from content marketing, brand strategies and affiliate marketing to truly make your customers connect and care about your brand.

The focus is on creating or identifying a strategy, and executing that strategy flawlessly. This requires that they work collaboratively with your internal team and help them implement the chosen strategy. It isn't a competitive environment where it is the ad agency versus the individual employee or employees. Instead, it is viewed through the lens of helping your team achieve the objectives that everyone collectively agrees are fundamental to the success of your business. This creates an entirely different environment where the consultant is viewed as a coach rather than as an intruder or someone who could possibly take your job.

This is why we constantly go out of our way to explain that we are a consultancy firm, not an ad agency. We offer clients what they need when they need it. It's not about adding another client to our portfolio but rather creating more success for the brands and people that we work with, which brings us back to the original point: the relevancy of ad agencies, or rather the lack thereof. If you have a large brand with a lot of SKU's and your team is overwhelmed, then bringing an excellent ad agency onboard makes sense. If your brand just needs some clarity and fresh guidance on how to reach your goals, hire a consultant.

Chapter 22: **The Power of YOU-centric Marketing**

One of the beautiful realities of YOU-centric digital marketing is that even the smallest brands can look larger than they are, and that is exactly what successful marketing does. It takes start-ups and makes them feel like they are on the path to epic success. It takes established brands and makes them feel personable and connected to their audience. While developing exceptional marketing strategies isn't easy, it is worth the effort because it puts your brand on a trajectory that is hard to match. It also makes it difficult for your competition to challenge your standing or market share because you have built a following of devoted and loyal fans.

Great marketing connects your brand with your customer's feelings because people buy identities and emotions. They buy items that represent their personality and uniqueness. They buy merchandise that makes them feel a certain way – powerful, sexy, confident. Think of the "power suit," the notion of a suit bringing out your inner lion has motivated many people to purchase. People buy to shift their attitudes and feel unstoppable. Your marketing needs to tap into these emotions or fulfill your customer's other needs, such as the need to feel significant (luxury items), the need for certainty (security and reliability), the need for variety (experiences and adventures), and the needs to contribute or grow. There is also the need to feel love or connection, which is why being part of something larger than yourself is compelling to so many consumers. These are the true needs that drive your customers to purchase; however, you can't uncover these needs if your focus is on your brand and not your customers. That is why the YOU-centric approach is so powerful, because it is about fulfilling your customer's needs, desires, aspirations and wants.

Think about Nordstrom. While they are known for outstanding customer service (fulfills the need for certainty), they are also brilliant marketers. They know exactly how to convey high quality (fulfills significance) as well as a deep knowledge of their customer's interests. Aspire to be the next Nordstrom. Allocate the necessary budget to position your brand for the long-term, work with experts that have an unrelenting passion for excellence, and come to terms with the time required to produce exceptional results. Aspire to be the next Patagonia that really understands the power of variety (adventure) for their customers. A YOU-centric approach always puts your customer's desires center-stage.

Chart a path of innovation that is also mission driven. Your brand can do all these things and more. Take the lid off of your expectations and be worthy of your customers' affections by over-delivering. Marketers have become convinced that it is the outside forces that are driving their brand results. The truth is, it is typically internal forces that have caused a disconnect with the customer. This doesn't mean you aren't able to correct, but it means that you need to earn back your customer's trust by making them the priority. It means you need to understand your ideal customer and cultivate a relationship that is all about them. Focus on meeting your customer's needs and seeing the results.

The other thing to remember is great YOU-centric marketing is fun. It gives your brand the opportunity to be authentic with your customers. It affords the chance to break through the noise because your brand is different. What's not fun about that? Successful marketers know that success comes from pleasing the customer. As a result, they think about different ways to improve the customer experience. Thinking differently about your customers is what all great brands do. They challenge themselves to provide something of value and make adding value a cornerstone of their business. The end result is that the customer feels both cared for and appreciated. What customer doesn't want that? And marketers couldn't ask for more.

If you do these things consistently, you will be a leader among brands, as well as your target audience. Your brand will stand out because so few have embraced a similar approach. Perhaps they don't understand it or they don't think it's necessary. Perhaps they view it as too difficult or too disconnected from traditional marketing. Perhaps it is just too new and different for them. Whatever the case, their misperception is your gain. YOU-centric marketers won't let the circumstances define them – they define the circumstances.

Here's to your success!

We would like to invite you to become part of our YOU-centric marketing family. Order a copy of my book for a friend and receive the following special bonus gifts:

1. Customer profile interview questionnaire that is unlike anything you have seen previously. This is the secret sauce of YOU-centric marketing (value $500.00)

2. One-on-one free marketing evaluation analysis and consultation (value $500.00)

If you feel like you don't know where to begin or just need a little guidance with creating a YOU-centric marketing plan for your business, we're here to help. Please feel free to contact us directly at the following:

www.thinkmediaconsult.com
Email: shebets@thinkmediaconsult.com
Ph: 720-213-8069

You can also reach me via social media:

Facebook: www.facebook.com/thinkmediaconsult
Instagram: @thinkmediaconsulting
Twitter: @ThinkMedia16

Please share this information with your friends and family, as we aim to help as many people and businesses as we can. You can purchase additional copies of this book at the following:

Amazon: www.amazon.com

Barnes & Noble: www.barnesandnoble.com

About the Author

Shahla Hebets has held executive management positions in media companies specializing in ecommerce, pay-per-click (SEM), search engine optimization (SEO) and other forms of digital marketing and advertising. With over two decades of experience developing digital marketing strategies for Fortune 500 companies to small businesses, Shahla founded Think Media Consulting in 2016 with a focus on helping healthy lifestyle brands grow. She lives in Denver, Colorado with her husband, two children, and dog.

Hearts to be HEARD

Giving a Voice to Creativity!

Wouldn't you love to help the physically, spiritually,
and mentally challenged?

Would you like to make a difference
in a child's life?

Imagine giving them:
confidence; self-esteem; pride; and self-respect.
Perhaps a legacy that lives on.

You see, that's what we do.
We give a voice to the creativity in their hearts,
for those who would otherwise not be heard.

Join us by going to

HeartstobeHeard.com

Help us, help others.

55810647R00076

Made in the USA
Middletown, DE
18 July 2019